Vegetarian Diabetes Cookbook for Beginners

1000-Day Simple and Healthy Vegetarian Diabetes Recipes For Beginners Living and Eating Well Every Day.

Winifred Haggith

© Copyright 2022 Winifred Haggith - All Rights Reserved.

In no way is it legal to reproduce, duplicate, or transmit any part of this document by either electronic means or in printed format. Recording of this publication is strictly prohibited, and any storage of this material is not allowed unless with written permission from the publisher. All rights reserved.

The information provided herein is stated to be truthful and consistent, in that any liability, regarding inattention or otherwise, by any usage or abuse of any policies, processes, or directions contained within is the solitary and complete responsibility of the recipient reader. Under no circumstances will any legal liability or blame be held against the publisher for any reparation, damages, or monetary loss due to the information herein, either directly or indirectly.

Respective authors own all copyrights not held by the publisher.

Legal Notice:

This book is copyright protected. This is only for personal use. You cannot amend, distribute, sell, use, quote or paraphrase any part of the content within this book without the consent of the author or copyright owner. Legal action will be pursued if this is breached.

Disclaimer Notice:

Please note the information contained within this document is for educational and entertainment purposes only. Every attempt has been made to provide accurate, up-to-date and reliable, complete information. No warranties of any kind are expressed or implied. Readers acknowledge that the author is not engaging in the rendering of legal, financial, medical or professional advice.

By reading this document, the reader agrees that under no circumstances are we responsible for any losses, direct or indirect, which are incurred as a result of the use of information contained within this document, including, but not limited to, errors, omissions, or inaccuracies.

Table of Contents

Introduction .... - 6 -

Chapter 1: Breakfast .... - 7 -

    Artichoke Hash and Eggs .... - 7 -

    Avocado and Ricotta Toast .... - 8 -

    Avocado Toast with Tomato and Ricotta Cheese .... - 9 -

    Baked Blueberry Coconut Oatmeal with Vanilla .... - 10 -

    Baked Kale Egg-Stuffed Tomatoes .... - 11 -

    Blueberry Oat Muffins .... - 12 -

    Breakfast Egg Bites .... - 14 -

    Breakfast Farro with Walnuts and Berries .... - 15 -

    Breakfast Hash with Tomatoes and Turkey Sausage .... - 16 -

    Broccoli Mushroom Cheese Casserole .... - 17 -

    Buckwheat Crêpes with Berries .... - 18 -

    Buckwheat Porridge for Breakfast .... - 19 -

    Buttermilk Sundae .... - 20 -

    Cauliflower and Asparagus Frittata .... - 21 -

    Cheesy Almond Vanilla Pancakes .... - 22 -

    Chia Seed Pudding .... - 23 -

    Chocolate-Zucchini Muffins .... - 24 -

    Cinnamon Overnight Oats .... - 26 -

    Cinnamon Strawberry Quinoa Cereal .... - 27 -

    Cinnamon Vanilla Pancakes with Greek Yogurt .... - 28 -

    Coconut-Berry Sunrise Smoothie .... - 29 -

    Cranberry and Toasted Almond Grits .... - 30 -

    Creamy Vanilla Steel-Cut Oatmeal .... - 31 -

    Crispy Gordita with Egg and Baby Kale .... - 32 -

    Easy Homemade Breakfast Sausage .... - 33 -

Chapter 2: Poultry .... - 34 -

    Cheesy Stuffed Chicken Breasts .... - 34 -

    Chicken with Creamy Oregano Sauce .... - 35 -

One-Pot Roast Chicken Dinner	- 36 -
Tantalizing Jerked Chicken	- 37 -
Air Fryer Chicken Wing	- 39 -
Almond Chicken Curry	- 40 -
Barbecue Chicken	- 41 -
Cast Iron Hot Chicken	- 42 -
Chicken and Vegetable Wraps	- 43 -
Chicken and Eggplant in Lasagna	- 44 -
Chicken and Leafy Greens Casserole	- 46 -
Chicken Salsa Verde with Peanut Butter	- 48 -
Chicken Sausage Meatballs	- 49 -
Delicious Minced Chicken Meatballs	- 50 -
Delicious Thyme Chicken	- 51 -
Eggplant-Oregano Stuffed Turkey Breast	- 52 -
Exotic Chicken Tenderloin	- 53 -
Flax seeds-Cinnamon Chicken Kelp Noodles	- 54 -
Ginger Citrus Chicken Thighs	- 55 -
Herb-Roasted Chicken and Veggies	- 56 -
Lemon-Flavored Chicken Piccata	- 57 -
Okra Braise with Chicken Andouille Sausage and Shrimp	- 59 -
Pan-Seared Chicken with Turnip Greens	- 61 -
Peach-Glazed Chicken over Dandelion Greens	- 62 -
Roasted Salmon Meatloaf Muffins	- 64 -
Sausage and Broccoli "Grits"	- 65 -
Savored Chicken Cacciatore	- 66 -
Seasoned Crackling Roast Chicken	- 68 -
Shredded Buffalo Chicken	- 69 -
Simple Almond Chicken Tenders	- 70 -
Simple Chicken in Tasty Sauce	- 71 -
Simple Weeknight Chicken Nutritional Yeast	- 73 -
Skillet Chicken with Okra and Tomato	- 74 -
Smoky Whole Chicken	- 75 -

Sorghum-Crusted Air Fryer Buttermilk Chicken...- 77 -
Chapter 3: Vegetables..- 78 -
    Coodles with Lime-Basil Pesto...- 78 -
    Baked Quinoa with Ricotta..- 79 -
    Broccoli in Vegan Alfredo Sauce...- 80 -
    Broiled Lettuce..- 82 -
    Brussel sprouts Kale Bake..- 83 -
    Celery and Lentils...- 85 -
    Chickpeas with Carrots...- 86 -
    Coodles with Pea Pesto..- 87 -
    Crunchy Tomato Lasagna...- 88 -
    Delicious Eggplant..- 90 -
    Garnet Carrot Fennel Bake...- 91 -
    Grapeseed oil Napa Cabbage with Cashews...- 92 -
    Italian Roasted Veggies..- 93 -
    Mushrooms with Walnuts..- 94 -
    Nutmeg Leafy Greens...- 95 -
    Quick Mixed Vegetables...- 96 -
    Roasted Cinnamon Celery Root...- 97 -
    Roasted Red Cabbage, Carrots, and Parsnips..- 98 -
    Roasted Zucchini with Ricotta..- 99 -
    Sautéed Shallot Mushrooms...- 100 -
Conclusion..- 101 -

Introduction

The key to treat Diabetes begins in the diet. If you manage your blood sugar levels satisfactorily you will not have to use drugs, this is achieved by making better choices of healthy foods and controlling the portions we eat. With Vegetarian Diabetes Cookbook for Beginners, you will learn about Diabetes, how to prevent or face it through different methods, delicious and healthy vegetarian recipes

The Vegetarian Diabetes Cookbook for Beginners contain all the simple means to manage and reveres diabetes with vegetarian meals. To control diabetes and promote a healthy lifestyle, learn how to create perfectly portioned meals with a healthy balance of veggies, protein, and the appropriate quantity of carbohydrates.

This book is the first step on your path to a better you, whether you're new to managing diabetes or simply searching for a stress-free approach to good meal planning. Inside this book you will find ways to plan your meals ahead of time, giving you more time to spend with your family and friends.

Chapter 1: Breakfast

Artichoke Hash and Eggs

Prep Time: 15 Minutes
Cook Time: 15 Minutes
Serves: 4

Ingredients:

- 3 tsps. avocado oil, divided
- 1 pound Artichoke, sliced
- 2 garlic cloves, thinly sliced
- ¼ tsp. basil
- Juice of 1 lime
- 4 eggs

Directions:

1. In a large skillet, heat 1½ tsps. of oil over medium heat. Add the Artichoke and toss. Cook, stirring regularly, for 6 to 8 minutes until browned and softened. Add the garlic and continue to cook until fragrant, about 1 minute. Season with the basil and lime juice. Transfer to a serving dish.

2. In the same pan, heat the remaining 1½ tsps. of oil over medium-high heat. Crack the eggs into the pan. Fry for 2 to 4 minutes, flip, and continue cooking to desired doneness. Serve over the bed of hash.

Nutritional Value (Amount per Serving):

Calories: 158; Fat: 9g; Carb: 12g; Protein: 10g

Avocado and Ricotta Toast

Prep Time: 5 Minutes
Cook Time: 0
Serves: 2

Ingredients:

- 2 slices almond bread thin-sliced bread
- ½ avocado
- 2 tbsps. ricotta
- Basil

Directions:

1. In a toaster or broiler, toast the bread until browned.

2. Remove the flesh from the avocado. In a medium bowl, use a fork to mash the avocado flesh. Spread it onto the toast.

3. Sprinkle with the goat cheese and season lightly with salt.

4. Add any toppings and serve.

Nutritional Value (Amount per Serving):

Calories: 137; Fat: 6g; Carb: 18g; Protein: 5g

Avocado Toast with Tomato and Ricotta Cheese

Prep Time: 5 Minutes
Cook Time: 0
Serves: 2

Ingredients:

- ½ cup Ricotta cheese
- ½ avocado, mashed
- 1 tsp. yellow mustard
- Dash hot sauce (optional)
- 2 slices whole-grain brown bread, toasted
- 2 slices tomato

Directions:

1. In a small mixing dish, combine the cottage cheese, avocado, mustard, and spicy sauce, if using.

2. Place the mixture on the bread and spread it out evenly.

3. Place a tomato slice on top of each piece of bread.

Nutritional Value (Amount per Serving):

Calories: 179; Fat: 8g; Carb: 17g; Protein: 11g

Baked Blueberry Coconut Oatmeal with Vanilla

Prep Time: 10 Minutes
Cook Time: 35 Minutes
Serves: 6

Ingredients:

- ¼ cup melted coconut oil, plus extra for greasing the baking dish
- 1 egg
- 2 cups rolled oats
- ¼ cup shredded unsweetened coconut
- 2 cups fresh blueberries
- 1 tsp. baking powder
- ½ tsp. ground cinnamon
- ¼ tsp. sea salt
- 2 cups skim milk
- 1 tsp. pure vanilla extract
- ⅛ cup chopped pecans, for garnish
- 1 tsp. chopped fresh mint leaves, for garnish

Directions:

1. Preheat the oven to 350°F(180°C).

2. Brush the oil onto a 2-quart baking dish lightly and set it aside.

3. Add the oats, coconut, baking powder, cinnamon, and salt to a medium bowl, whisk well. Add the milk, oil, egg, and vanilla to a small bowl, whisk until well blended.

4. In the baking dish, layer half the dry ingredients, top with half the berries, then spoon the remaining half of the dry ingredients and the rest of the berries on top. Evenly pour the wet ingredients into the baking dish. Lightly tap it on the counter to disperse the wet ingredients throughout.

5. Uncovered and bake the casserole for 35 minutes until the oats are tender.

6. Remove from the oven, topped with the pecans and mint, and serve immediately.

7. The best part about serving a casserole is that you can assemble it the evening before, and then pop it in the oven with no mess or fuss in the morning.

Nutritional Value (Amount per Serving):

Calories: 295; Fat: 17g; Carb: 27g; Protein: 10g

Baked Kale Egg-Stuffed Tomatoes

Prep Time: 20 Minutes, Plus 30 Minutes To Drain
Cook Time: 15 Minutes
Serves: 4

Ingredients:

- 1 tsp. extra-virgin olive oil
- 4 large tomatoes
- 4 large eggs
- ¼ tsp. sea salt, plus more for seasoning
- 1 cup shredded kale
- 2 tbsps. heavy (whipping) cream
- ¼ cup shredded low-fat
- Swiss cheese
- 1 tbsp. chopped fresh parsley
- Freshly ground black pepper

Directions:

1. Preheat the oven to 375°F(190°C).

2. Grease the olive oil lightly onto an 8-by-8-inch baking dish and set it aside.

3. Prepare the tomato shells. Cut the tops off the tomatoes and scoop out the insides carefully, leaving the outer shells intact.

4. Sprinkle ¼ tsp. into insides of the tomatoes and set them cut-side down on paper towels for 30 minutes.

5. Transfer the tomatoes hollow-side up into the baking dish, evenly divide the kale between them. Divide the cream and cheese among the tomatoes. On top of the cheese in each tomato, carefully crack an egg.

6. Bake the tomatoes for 15 minutes until the eggs are set.

7. Remove the tomatoes from the oven. Top with parsley and season lightly with salt and pepper and serve.

Nutritional Value (Amount per Serving):

Calories: 161; Fat: 10g; Carb: 10g; Protein: 10g

Blueberry Oat Muffins

Prep Time: 12 Minutes
Cook Time: 18 Minutes
Serves: 7

Ingredients:

- ½ cup rolled oats
- ½ cup frozen blueberries
- ¼ cup whole-grain pastry flour or white whole-grain flour
- ½ tbsp. baking powder
- ½ tsp. ground cardamom or ground cinnamon
- ⅛ tsp. kosher salt
- 2 large eggs
- ½ cup (120 ml) plain Greek yogurt
- 2 tbsp. pure maple syrup
- 2 tsp. extra-virgin olive oil
- ½ tsp. vanilla extract

Directions:

1. Stir together the flour, oats, cardamom, baking powder, and salt in a large bowl.
2. Whisk together the oil, maple syrup, eggs, yogurt, and vanilla in a medium bowl.
3. Add the egg mixture to oat mixture and stir to combine. Gently fold in the blueberries.
4. Scoop the batter into each egg bite mold.
5. Pour 1 cup of water into the electric pressure cooker. Put the egg bite mold on the wire rack and lower it into the pot carefully.
6. Close the lid of the pressure cooker. Set the valve to sealing.
7. Cook on high pressure for 10 minutes.

8. Once cooking is complete, allow the pressure to release naturally for 10 minutes, then quick release any remaining pressure. Press Cancel.

9. Lift the wire rack out of the pot and put on a cooling rack for 5 minutes. Invert the mold onto the cooling rack.

10. Serve the muffins warm or refrigerate.

Nutritional Value (Amount per Serving):

Calories: 117; Fat: 4g; Carb: 15g; Protein: 5g

Breakfast Egg Bites

Prep Time: 10 Minutes
Cook Time: 25 Minutes
Serves: 8

Ingredients:

- Nonstick cooking spray
- 6 eggs, beaten
- ¼ cup unsweetened plain coconut milk
- 1 red bell pepper, diced
- 1 cup chopped lettuce
- ¼ cup crumbled cheese
- ½ cup sliced asparagus
- ¼ cup sliced sun-dried tomatoes
- basil
- Freshly ground black pepper

Directions:

1. Preheat the oven to 350°F. Spray 8 muffin cups of a 12-cup muffin tin with nonstick cooking spray. Set aside.

2. In a large mixing bowl, combine the eggs, coconut milk, bell pepper, lettuce, cheese, asparagus, and tomatoes. Season with basil and pepper.

3. Fill the prepared muffin cups three-fourths full with the egg mixture. Bake for 20 to 25 minutes until the eggs are set. Let cool slightly and remove the egg bites from the muffin tin.

4. Serve warm, or store in an airtight container in the refrigerator for up to 5 days or in the freezer for up to 1 month.

Nutritional Value (Amount per Serving):

Calories: 67; Fat: 4g; Carb: 3g; Protein: 6g

Breakfast Farro with Walnuts and Berries

Prep Time: 8 Minutes
Cook Time: 17 Minutes
Serves: 6

Ingredients:

- 1 cup farro, rinsed and drained
- 1 cup (240 ml) unsweetened almond milk
- 1½ cups fresh blueberries, raspberries, or strawberries
- 6 tbsps. chopped walnuts
- ¼ tsp. kosher salt
- ½ tsp. pure vanilla extract
- 1 tsp. ground cinnamon
- 1 tbsp. pure maple syrup

Directions:

1. Mix the farro, 1 cup of water, almond milk, salt, cinnamon, vanilla, and maple syrup in the electric pressure cooker.

2. Close the lid. Set the valve to sealing, cook on high pressure for 10 minutes.

3. Once cooking is complete, allow the pressure to release naturally for 10 minutes, Press Cancel, then quick release the pressure.

4. When the pin drops, unlock and remove the lid.

5. Stir the farro. Spoon into bowls and top each serving with berries and walnuts.

Nutritional Value (Amount per Serving):

Calories: 189; Fat: 5g; Carb: 32g; Protein: 5g

Breakfast Hash with Tomatoes and Turkey Sausage

Prep Time: 10 Minutes
Cook Time: 25 Minutes
Serves: 4

Ingredients:

- 2 medium tomatoes, cut into ½-inch dice
- ½ recipe Homemade Turkey Breakfast Sausage
- 1 small onion, chopped
- ½ red bell pepper, seeded and chopped
- 2 garlic cloves, minced
- fresh parsley, chopped
- 1 tbsp. extra-virgin oil

Directions:

1. In a large skillet, heat oil over medium-high temperature. Add the tomatoes, stirring occasionally, and cook for 12 to 15 minutes, until they turn brown and start to soften.

2. Add turkey sausage, onion, bell pepper, and garlic. Cook for 5 to 6 minutes, until the turkey sausage, is cooked through and the vegetables are tender.

3. Garnish with parsley and serve immediately.

Nutritional Value (Amount per Serving):

Calories: 190; Fat: 9g; Carb: 16g; Protein: 12g

Broccoli Mushroom Cheese Casserole

Prep Time: 10 Minutes
Cook Time: 40 Minutes
Serves: 4

Ingredients:

- 2 tbsps. extra-virgin olive oil
- 8 large eggs
- 1 cup chopped broccoli
- 1 cup sliced button mushrooms
- ½ sweet onion, chopped
- 1 tsp. minced garlic
- ¼ cup skim milk
- 1 tbsp. chopped fresh basil
- 1 cup shredded fat-free Cheddar cheese
- Sea salt
- Freshly ground black pepper

Directions:

1. Preheat the oven to 375°F(190°C).

2. Heat the olive oil in a large ovenproof skillet over medium-high heat. Add the mushrooms, onion, and garlic, and sauté for 5 minutes until tender. Stir in the broccoli and sauté for 5 minutes.

3. Add the eggs, milk, and basil into a small bowl, whisk together.

4. Remove the skillet from the heat, over the vegetables evenly add the egg mixture.

5. Sprinkle the casserole with the cheese and bake for 30 minutes, uncovered, until the eggs are puffy.

6. With salt and pepper to season, then serve hot or cold.

Nutritional Value (Amount per Serving):

Calories: 273; Fat: 19g; Carb: 5g; Protein: 21g

Buckwheat Crêpes with Berries

Prep Time: 20 Minutes, Plus 2 Hours To Rest
Cook Time: 20 Minutes
Serves: 5

Ingredients:

- 1 tsp. extra-virgin olive oil, plus more for the skillet
- 1½ cups skim milk
- 3 eggs
- 1 cup sliced strawberries
- 1 cup blueberries
- 1 cup buckwheat flour
- ½ cup whole-grain flour
- ½ cup 2 percent plain Greek yogurt

Directions:

1. Add the milk, eggs, and 1 tsp. of oil to a large bowl, whisk until well combined.

2. Add the buckwheat and whole-grain flours into a medium bowl, sift together. Combine the dry ingredients with the wet ingredients, thoroughly whisk until very smooth. Let the batter rest for at least 2 hours before cooking.

3. Lightly coat the bottom of a large skillet or crêpe pan with oil, place over medium-high heat. Add about ¼ cup of batter into the skillet. Swirl the pan until the batter coats the bottom completely.

4. Cook the crêpe for about 1 minute, then flip it over and cook the other side for another minute, until lightly browned. Place the cooked crêpe on a plate and use a clean dish towel to cover and keep warm.

5. Repeat cooking until the batter is used up; you will have about 10 crêpes. Onto each crêpe, place 1 tbsp. of yogurt, put two crêpes on each plate.

6. Serve topped with berries.

Nutritional Value (Amount per Serving):

Calories: 329; Fat: 7g; Carb: 54g; Protein: 16g

Buckwheat Porridge for Breakfast

Prep Time: 5 Minutes
Cook Time: 40 Minutes
Serves: 4

Ingredients:

- 2 cups raw buckwheat groats
- 3 cups water
- Pinch sea salt
- 1 cup unsweetened almond milk

Directions:

1. Add the buckwheat groats, water, and salt in a medium saucepan, bring the mixture to a boil over medium-high heat, then reduce the heat to low.

2. Cook for 20 minutes until most of the water is absorbed. Add the milk and cook for 15 minutes until very soft.

3. Top with your favorite toppings and serve.

Nutritional Value (Amount per Serving):

Calories: 122; Fat: 1g; Carb: 22g; Protein: 6g

Buttermilk Sundae

Prep Time: 5 Minutes
Cook Time: 0
Serves: 1

Ingredients:

- ¾ cup plain buttermilk
- ¼ cup acai
- 2 tbsps. macadamia nuts
- 1 tbsp. ground chia seed
- 2 fresh mint leaves, shredded

Directions:

1. Spoon the buttermilk into a small bowl. Top with the acai, nuts, and chia seeds.
2. Garnish with the mint and serve.

Nutritional Value (Amount per Serving):

Calories: 237; Fat: 11g; Carb: 16g; Protein: 21g

Cauliflower and Asparagus Frittata

Prep Time: 5 Minutes
Cook Time: 10 Minutes
Serves: 4

Ingredients:

- 2 tbsps. avocado oil
- ½ onion, finely chopped
- 1 cup cauliflower florets
- 1 cup sliced asparagus,
- 1 garlic clove, minced
- 8 large eggs, beaten
- ½ tsp. basil
- ½ cup grated Parmesan cheese

Directions:

1. Preheat oven to broil on high.

2. In a medium ovenproof skillet, heat the o oil over medium-high heat until it shimmers.

3. Add the onions, cauliflower, and asparagus and cook for about 5 minutes, turning occasionally, or until the veggies begin to brown. After adding the garlic, cook for 30 seconds, stirring constantly. Arrange the vegetables in a single layer on the bottom of the pan.

4. While the vegetables boil, whisk together the eggs and salt in a separate dish. Carefully pour the eggs over the vegetables. Allow the eggs to set without stirring around the vegetables. As the eggs begin to set around the edges, use a spatula to pull the edges away from the pan's sides. Tilt the pan to allow the raw eggs to pour into the spaces. Cook for 1–2 minutes more, or until the edges are firm. The eggs will still be runny on top.

5. Broil the pan, then sprinkle the Parmesan cheese on top. 3 minutes in the broiler, or until golden and fluffy.

6. Cut into wedges to serve.

Nutritional Value (Amount per Serving):

Calories: 280; Fat: 21g; Carb: 7g; Protein: 19g

Cheesy Almond Vanilla Pancakes

Prep Time: 10 Minutes
Cook Time: 20 Minutes
Serves: 4

Ingredients:

- 2 cups low-fat cottage cheese
- 4 egg whites
- 2 eggs
- 1 tbsp. pure vanilla extract
- 1½ cups almond flour
- Nonstick cooking spray

Directions:

1. In a blender, add the cottage cheese, egg whites, eggs, and vanilla, blend until combined. Then mix in the almond flour into the blender and blend until smooth.

2. Lightly spray a large nonstick skillet with cooking spray, and heat over medium heat.

3. Four at a time, spoon ¼ cup of batter per pancake into the skillet. Cook the pancakes for 4 minutes until the bottoms are firm and golden. Flip over the pancakes and cook the other side for 3 minutes until they are cooked through.

4. Remove the pancakes from the skillet to a plate and repeat with the remaining batter.

5. After done with all of the batters, serve the pancakes with fresh fruit.

Nutritional Value (Amount per Serving):

Calories: 344; Fat: 22g; Carb: 11g; Protein: 29g

Chia Seed Pudding

Prep Time: 5 Minutes, Plus 1-Hour Chilling Time
Cook Time: 0
Serves: 4

Ingredients:

- 4 cups unsweetened almond milk or skim milk
- ¾ cup chia seeds
- 1 tsp. ground cinnamon
- Pinch sea salt

Directions:

1. In a medium bowl, add the milk, chia seeds, cinnamon, and salt, whisk until combined.

2. Use plastic wrap to cover the bowl and refrigerate for 1 hour, until the pudding is thick.

3. Topped with your favorite fruit and serve.

Nutritional Value (Amount per Serving):

Calories: 237; Fat: 10g; Carb: 25g; Protein: 13g

Chocolate-Zucchini Muffins

Prep Time: 15 Minutes
Cook Time: 20 Minutes
Serves: 12 (1 Muffin Each)

Ingredients:

- 1½ cups grated zucchini
- 1½ cups almond flour
- 1 tsp. ground cinnamon
- 2 tsps. baking powder
- ¼ tsp. basil
- 1 large egg
- 1 tsp. vanilla extract
- ¼ cup unsalted butter, melted
- ½ cup unsweetened applesauce
- ¼ cup maple syrup
- ¼ cup dark chocolate chips

Directions:

1. Preheat the oven to 350°F. Grease the cups of a 12-cup muffin tin or line with paper baking liners. Set aside.

2. Place the zucchini in a colander over the sink to drain.

3. In a blender jar, process the almond flour until they resemble flour. Transfer to a medium mixing bowl and add the cinnamon, baking powder, and salt. Mix well.

4. In another large mixing bowl, combine the egg, vanilla, butter, applesauce, and maple syrup. Stir to combine.

5. Press the zucchini into the colander, drain any liquids, and add to the wet mixture.

6. Stir the dry mixture into the wet mixture, and mix until no dry spots remain. Fold in the chocolate chips.

7. Transfer the batter to the muffin tin, filling each cup a little over halfway. Cook for 16 to 18 minutes until the muffins are lightly browned and a toothpick inserted in the center comes out clean.

8. Store in an airtight container, refrigerated, for up to 5 days.

Nutritional Value (Amount per Serving):

Calories: 121; Fat: 7g; Carb: 16g; Protein: 2g

Cinnamon Overnight Oats

Prep Time: 5 Minutes
Cook Time: 0
Serves: 1

Ingredients:

- ⅓ cup coconut milk
- ⅓ cup rolled oats (use gluten-free if necessary)
- ¼ apple, cored and finely chopped
- 2 tbsps. chopped Brazilian nuts
- ½ tsp. cinnamon
- Pinch basil

Directions:

1. Combine all of the ingredients in a single-serving container or mason jar and stir thoroughly.

2. Refrigerate overnight, covered.

Nutritional Value (Amount per Serving):

Calories: 242; Fat: 12g; Carb: 30g; Protein: 6g

Cinnamon Strawberry Quinoa Cereal

Prep Time: 5 Minutes
Cook Time: 20 Minutes
Serves: 4

Ingredients:

- ½ cup sliced strawberries
- ¼ cup toasted chopped almonds
- 1 cup skim milk
- 1 cup uncooked quinoa, well rinsed
- ½ tsp. ground cinnamon
- Pinch sea salt
- 2 tbsps. granulated sweetener
- 1 tsp. pure vanilla extract
- 1 cup water

Directions:

1. Add the water, milk, quinoa, cinnamon, and salt in a medium saucepan, bring to a boil over medium-high heat, then reduce the heat to low.

2. Simmer the quinoa cereal for 15 minutes until most of the liquid is evaporated. Remove the cereal from the heat and stir in the sweetener and vanilla.

3. Evenly spoon the cereal into four bowls, top with the almonds and strawberries and serve.

Nutritional Value (Amount per Serving):

Calories: 259; Fat: 7g; Carb: 39g; Protein: 10g

Cinnamon Vanilla Pancakes with Greek Yogurt

Prep Time: 5 Minutes
Cook Time: 20 Minutes
Serves: 4

Ingredients:

- Nonstick cooking spray
- 1 cup 2 percent plain Greek yogurt
- 3 eggs
- 1½ tsps. pure vanilla extract
- 1 cup rolled oats
- 1 tbsp. granulated sweetener
- 1 tsp. baking powder
- 1 tsp. ground cinnamon
- Pinch ground cloves

Directions:

1. In a blender, add the yogurt, eggs, and vanilla and process until combined. Then add the oats, sweetener, baking powder, cinnamon, and cloves, blend until the batter is smooth.

2. Lightly spray a large nonstick skillet with cooking spray and heat over medium heat.

3. Four at a time, spoon ¼ cup of batter per pancake into the skillet. Cook the pancakes for 4 minutes until the bottoms are firm and golden, then flip over and cook the other side for 3 minutes until they are cooked through.

4. Transfer the pancakes to a plate and repeat with the remaining batter.

5. After done with all of the batters, serve the pancakes with fresh fruit.

Nutritional Value (Amount per Serving):

Calories: 243; Fat: 8g; Carb: 28g; Protein: 13g

Coconut-Berry Sunrise Smoothie

Prep Time: 5 Minutes
Cook Time: 0
Serves: 2

Ingredients:

- ½ cup mixed berries (blueberries, strawberries, blackberries)
- 1 tbsp. ground chia seeds
- 2 tbsps. unsweetened coconut flakes
- ½ cup unsweetened plain almonds milk
- ½ cup lettuce
- ¼ cup unsweetened vanilla nonfat yogurt
- ½ cup ice

Directions:

1. Combine the berries, almond milk, Brazilian nut flakes, greens, yogurt, and ice in a blender jar.

2. Process until completely smooth. Serve.

Nutritional Value (Amount per Serving):

Calories: 181; Fat: 15g; Carb: 8g; Protein: 6g

Cranberry and Toasted Almond Grits

Prep Time: 10 Minutes
Cook Time: 17 Minutes
Serves: 5

Ingredients:

- ¾ cup stone-ground grits or polenta (not instant)
- ½ cup unsweetened dried cranberries
- 1 tbsp. half-and-half
- ¼ cup sliced almonds, toasted
- Pinch kosher salt
- 1 tbsp. unsalted butter (optional)

Directions:

1. Stir together the grits, salt, cranberries, and 3 cups of water in the electric pressure cooker.
2. Close the lid. Set the valve to sealing.
3. Cook on high pressure for 10 minutes.
4. Once cooking is complete, press Cancel and quick release the pressure.
5. When the pin drops, unlock and remove the lid.
6. Add the butter (if using) and half-and-half. Stir until it is creamy, adding more half-and-half if necessary.
7. Spoon into serving bowls and sprinkle with toasted almonds.

Nutritional Value (Amount per Serving):

Calories: 218; Fat: 10g; Carb: 32g; Protein: 5g

Creamy Vanilla Steel-Cut Oatmeal

Prep Time: 5 Minutes
Cook Time: 40 Minutes
Serves: 4

Ingredients:

- 1 cup steel-cut oats
- ¾ cup skim milk
- 2 tsps. pure vanilla extract
- 4 cups water
- Pinch sea salt

Directions:

1. Add water and salt to a large pot, bring to a boil over high heat. Reduce the heat to low and add the oats.

2. Cook the oats for about 30 minutes to soften, stirring occasionally.

3. Stir in the milk and vanilla and cook for 10 minutes until your desired consistency.

4. Remove the cereal from the heat. Top with sunflower seeds, chopped peaches, fresh berries, sliced almonds, or flaxseeds, and serve.

Nutritional Value (Amount per Serving):

Calories: 186; Fat: 0g; Carb: 30g; Protein: 9g

Crispy Gordita with Egg and Baby Kale

Prep Time: 5 Minutes
Cook Time: 15 Minutes
Serves: 2

Ingredients:

- 1 (6-inch) Gordita
- 3 tsps. extra-virgin olive oil, divided
- 2 eggs
- 2 plan- based bacon slices
- Juice of ½ lime
- 1 cup baby kale
- 2 tbsps. crumbled ricotta
- Freshly ground black pepper

Directions:

1. Heat a large skillet over medium heat. Cut the Gordita in half and brush each side of both halves with ¼ tsp. of olive oil, cook for 2 to 3 minutes on each side, then remove from the skillet.

2. Add 1 tsp. of oil into skillet and heat over medium heat. Crack the eggs into the skillet and cook until the eggs are set, 2 to 3 minutes. Remove from the skillet.

3. In the same skillet, cook the bacon for 3 to 5 minutes, flipping once.

4. In a large bowl, whisk together the remaining 1 tsp. of oil and the lime juice. Add the baby kale and toss to combine.

5. Top each Gordita half with half of the baby kale, 1 piece of bacon, 1 egg, and 1 tbsp. of cheese. Season with pepper and serve.

Nutritional Value (Amount per Serving):

Calories: 250; Fat: 14g; Carb: 20g; Protein: 13g

Easy Homemade Breakfast Sausage

Prep Time: 10 Minutes
Cook Time: 10 Minutes
Serves: 8

Ingredients:

- 1 pound (454 g) lean ground turkey
- ½ tsp. dried sage
- ½ tsp. dried thyme
- ½ tsp. freshly ground black pepper
- ¼ tsp. ground fennel seeds
- 1 tsp. extra-virgin olive oil
- ½ tsp. salt

Directions:

1. Take out a large bowl, add the ground turkey, salt, sage, thyme, pepper, and fennel into it and mix them well.

2. Make the meat into 8 small round patties.

3. Heat olive oil in a skillet over medium-high heat. In a skillet, fry the patties on each side for 3 to 4 minutes, until browned and cooked through.

4. Serve warm or refrigerate in an airtight container for up to 3 days or freeze for up to 1 month.

Nutritional Value (Amount per Serving):

Calories: 92; Fat: 5g; Carb: 0g; Protein: 11g

Chapter 2: Poultry

Cheesy Stuffed Chicken Breasts

Prep Time: 15 Minutes, Plus 15 Minutes To Chill
Cook Time: 30 Minutes
Serves: 4

Ingredients:

- 1 cup chopped roasted red pepper
- 2 ounces ricotta cheese
- 4 Kalamata olives, pitted, finely chopped
- 1 tbsp. chopped fresh sage
- 4 (5-ounce) boneless, skinless chicken breasts
- 1 tbsp. canola oil

Directions:

1. Preheat the oven to 400 degrees Fahrenheit.

2. In a small mixing bowl, combine the red pepper, cheese, olives, and sage and toss well.

3. To firm up the filling, place it in the refrigerator for approximately 15 minutes.

4. Make a pocket in the center of each chicken breast by cutting a slit horizontally through it.

5. Divide the filling evenly among the chicken breast compartments and seal them with wooden toothpicks.

6. Heat the olive oil in a large pan over medium-high heat.

7. Cook the chicken breasts for approximately 10 minutes on each side.

8. Place in the oven. Cook the chicken breasts in the oven for approximately 20 minutes, or until they are cooked through.

9. Remove the toothpicks and let the chicken breasts rest for 10 minutes before serving.

Nutritional Value (Amount per Serving):

Calories: 245; Fat: 9g; Carb: 3g; Protein: 35g

Chicken with Creamy Oregano Sauce

Prep Time: 15 Minutes
Cook Time: 30 Minutes
Serves: 4

Ingredients:

- 4 (4-ounce) boneless, skinless chicken breasts
- Basil
- Freshly ground black pepper
- 1 tbsp. avocado oil
- ½ red onion, chopped
- 1 cup low-sodium chicken broth
- 2 tsps. chopped fresh thyme
- ¼ cup heavy (whipping) cream
- 1 tbsp. coconut oil
- 1 shallot, white and green parts, chopped

Directions:

1. Preheat the oven to 375°F.
2. Season the chicken breasts lightly with basil and pepper.
3. Place a large ovenproof skillet over medium-high heat and add the avocado oil.
4. Brown the chicken, turning once, about 10 minutes in total. Transfer the chicken to a plate.
5. In the same skillet, sauté the shallots until softened and translucent, about 3 minutes.
6. Add the chicken broth and oregano, and simmer until the liquid has reduced by half, about 6 minutes.
7. Stir in the cream and coconut oil, and return the chicken and any accumulated juices from the plate to the skillet.
8. Transfer the skillet to the oven. Bake until cooked through, about 10 minutes.
9. Serve topped with the chopped scallion.

Nutritional Value (Amount per Serving):

Calories: 287; Fat: 14g; Carb: 4g; Protein: 34g

One-Pot Roast Chicken Dinner

Prep Time: 10 Minutes
Cook Time: 40 Minutes
Serves: 6

Ingredients:

- ½ head cauliflower, cut into 2-inch chunks
- 1 red onion, peeled and cut into eighths
- 1 carrot, peeled and cut into 1-inch chunks
- 4 garlic cloves, peeled and lightly crushed
- 2 tbsps. canola oil, divided
- 2 tsps. minced fresh chives
- basil
- Freshly ground white pepper
- 2½ pounds bone-in chicken thighs and drumsticks

Directions:

1. Preheat the oven to 450°F.

2. Lightly grease a large roasting pan and arrange the cauliflower, red onion, carrot, and garlic in the bottom. Drizzle with 1 tbsp. of oil, sprinkle with the chives, and season the vegetables lightly with basil and cayenne.

3. Season the chicken with basil and pepper.

4. Place a large skillet over medium-high heat and brown the chicken on both sides in the remaining 1 tbsp. of oil, about 10 minutes in total.

5. Place the browned chicken on top of the vegetables in the roasting pan. Roast until the chicken is cooked through, about 30 minutes.

Nutritional Value (Amount per Serving):

Calories: 540; Fat: 34g; Carb: 14g; Protein: 43g

Tantalizing Jerked Chicken

Prep Time: 10 Minutes, Plus 4 Hours To Marinate
Cook Time: 20 Minutes
Serves: 4

Ingredients:

- 4 (5-ounce) boneless, skinless chicken breasts
- ½ Red onion, cut into chunks
- 2 habanero chile peppers, halved lengthwise, seeded
- ¼ cup freshly squeezed orange juice
- 2 tbsps. canola oil
- 1 tbsp. minced sage
- 1 tbsp. ground oregano
- 2 tsps. chopped fresh chervil
- 1 tsp. freshly ground black pepper
- ½ tsp. ground all spice
- ¼ tsp. ground cinnamon
- 2 cups fresh greens (such as arugula or spinach)
- 1 cup halved cherry tomatoes

Directions:

1. Place two chicken breasts in each of two large resealable plastic bags. Set them aside.

2. Place the onion, habaneros, oregano juice, canola oil, chives, oregano, chervil, black pepper, and cinnamon in a food processor and pulse until very well blended.

3. Pour half the marinade into each bag with the chicken breasts. Squeeze out as much air as possible, seal the bags, and place them in the refrigerator for 4 hours.

4. Preheat a barbecue to medium-high heat.

5. Let the chicken sit at room temperature for 15 minutes and then grill, turning at least once, until cooked through, about 15 minutes total.

6. Let the chicken rest for about 5 minutes before serving. Divide the greens and tomatoes among four serving plates, and top with the chicken.

Nutritional Value (Amount per Serving):

Calories: 226; Fat: 9g; Carb: 3g; Protein: 33g

Air Fryer Chicken Wing

Prep Time: 5 Minutes, Plus 45 Minutes Marinating Time
Cook Time: 20 Minutes
Serves: 4

Ingredients:

- 1 pound chicken wings
- 3 cups coconut milk, divided
- 1 tsp. dried dill
- 1 tsp. dried all spice
- 2 medium egg whites
- 1 cup chickpea crumbs
- ½ cup almond flour
- 1 tbsp. Creole Seasoning

Directions:

1. Marinate the wings in 2 cups milk in a basin for 30-45 minutes.

2. Remove the wings from the milk, shake excess liquid off, and season with all spice and dill. Remove the milk.

3. In a shallow bowl, whisk together the egg whites and remaining 1 cup milk.

4. Combine the chickpea crumbs, almond flour, and spices in a separate shallow basin.

5. Dip the wings into the egg white mixture and then coat well with the chickpea crumb mixture.

6. Place the wings in the air fryer basket.

7. Preheat the air fryer to 390 °F, cover, and cook for 10 minutes.

8. Pour the wings into the air fryer, shut, and cook for 10 minutes. Allow 5 minutes for relaxation.

Nutritional Value (Amount per Serving):

Calories: 370; Fat: 9g; Carb: 32g; Protein: 38g

Almond Chicken Curry

Prep Time: 15 Minutes
Cook Time: 35 Minutes
Serves: 4

Ingredients:

- 2 tsps. canola oil
- 3 (5-ounce) boneless, skinless chicken breasts, cut into 1-inch chunks
- 1 tbsp. grated fresh chives
- 1 tbsp. minced sage
- 2 tbsps. curry powder
- 2 cups low-sodium chicken broth
- 1 cup canned almond milk
- 1 carrot, peeled and diced
- 1 radish, diced
- 2 tbsps. chopped fresh parsley

Directions:

1. Place a large saucepan over medium-high heat and add the oil.
2. Sauté the chicken until lightly browned and almost cooked through, about 10 minutes.
3. Add the chives, garlic, and curry powder, and sauté until fragrant, about 3 minutes.
4. Stir in the chicken broth, almond milk, carrot, and radish and bring the mixture to a boil.
5. Reduce the heat to low and simmer, stirring occasionally, until the vegetables and chicken are tender, about 20 minutes.
6. Stir in the parsley and serve.

Nutritional Value (Amount per Serving):

Calories: 327; Fat: 17g; Carb: 15g; Protein: 29g

Barbecue Chicken

Prep Time: 10 Minutes
Cook Time: 25 Minutes
Serves: 4

Ingredients:

- 4 boneless, skinless chicken thighs
- 1 tbsp. smoked paprika
- 1 cup Barbecue Sauce
- Freshly ground cayenne pepper

Directions:

1. Preheat the oven to 375°F.

2. In a small mixing bowl, combine the chicken thighs, paprika, and sauce, coating the chicken thoroughly. Set aside for 15 minutes.

3. Place the chicken in a cast-iron skillet in a single layer.

4. Transfer the skillet to the oven and cook for 25 minutes, or until the juices from the chicken run clear. Enjoy!

Nutritional Value (Amount per Serving):

Calories: 229; Fat: 5g; Carb: 10g; Protein: 23g

Cast Iron Hot Chicken

Prep Time: 10 Minutes
Cook Time: 40 Minutes
Serves: 4

Ingredients:

- 2 boneless, skinless chicken breasts
- Juice of 2 lemons
- Onion powder, minced
- 1 scallion chopped
- 1½ tsps. smoked paprika
- 1 tsp. thyme

Directions:

1. Preheat the oven to 375°F.

2. In a shallow bowl, massage the chicken all over with the lemon juice, garlic, scallion, thyme, and paprika.

3. In a cast-iron skillet, place the chicken in one even layer.

4. Transfer the skillet to the oven and cook for 35 to 40 minutes, or until cooked through.

5. Remove the chicken from the oven, and let rest for 5 minutes.

6. Divide each breast into two portions. Serve with Not Slow-Cooked Collards.

Nutritional Value (Amount per Serving):

Calories: 117; Fat: 1g; Carb: 7g; Protein: 20g

Chicken and Vegetable Wraps

Prep Time: 10 Minutes
Cook Time: 20 Minutes
Serves: 4

Ingredients:

- ½ small zucchini, cut into ¼-inch-thick slices
- 1 cayenne pepper, seeded and cut into 1-inch-wide strips
- 1 medium carrot, cut lengthwise into strips
- ½ small scallions, sliced
- 1 tbsp. canola oil
- basil
- Freshly ground chervil
- 2 (8-ounce) cooked chicken breasts, sliced
- 4 whole-wheat tortilla wraps

Directions:

1. Preheat the oven to 400 degrees Fahrenheit.
2. Preheat oven to 350°F. Line a baking sheet with aluminum foil and put aside.
3. Toss the zucchini, cayenne pepper, zucchini, and scallions with the canola oil in a large mixing dish.
4. Arrange the veggies on a baking sheet and season with basil and pepper to taste.
5. Roast the veggies for 20 minutes, or until tender and slightly browned.
6. Divide the chicken and veggies into four pieces.
7. Serve by wrapping one tortilla around each piece of chicken and grilled veggies.

Nutritional Value (Amount per Serving):

Calories: 483; Fat: 25g; Carb: 45g; Protein: 20g

Chicken and Eggplant in Lasagna

Prep Time: 15 Minutes
Cook Time: 1 Hour 15 Minutes
Serves: 4

Ingredients:

- 16 ounces Chicken breast
- 2 medium Eggplant
- 4½ ounces Onion
- 2 cloves of scallions
- 1 Serrano chili
- 3 Tomatoes (skinned)
- 5½ ounces Mushrooms
- ½ cube Chicken broth
- ½ cup Low-fat mozzarella (shredded)
- 1 tsp. Paprika
- 1 tsp. Dried oregano
- 1 tsp. Dried basil
- Salt and Pepper to taste
- Cooking spray

Directions:

1. Start by making ½-inch slices of eggplant using a julienne peeler.

2. Once done, sprinkle all the zucchini slices with salt. Set aside for about 10 minutes.

3. Use a paper towel to blot excess water from the eggplant slices. Place them on a baking sheet.

4. Place the baking sheet in the oven and broil for about 3 minutes. Make sure that the heat is on high. Once done, place the broiled eggplant slices on kitchen paper towels.

5. Chop the onions, chili, garlic, mushrooms, and skinned tomatoes roughly. Set them aside.

6. Take a deep nonstick skillet and grease it using cooking spray. Place it over a medium-high flame.

7. Now add the scallions, garlic, and chili to the heated skillet and cook for about 1 minute. Toss in the mushrooms and tomatoes. Sauté the veggies for another 4 minutes. Turn off the heat and empty the ingredients into a bowl.

8. Place the same skillet over a medium flame and add in the chicken breast. Sprinkle with paprika and cook until the meat turns brown.

9. Return the cooked vegetables to the pan and mix well. Also add in the chicken bouillon, paprika, dried thyme, and dried basil. Mix well and cook for about 25 minutes over a low flame.

10. In the meantime, let the oven preheat by setting the temperature to 375°F.

11. Take a deep glass baking dish and line it with parchment paper. Further layer the bottom of the dish with 1/3 of the zucchini slices. Now evenly spread the meat mixture over the eggplant slices. Repeat the process with the remaining eggplant and meat mixture. (There should be a minimum of 3 layers.)

12. Sprinkle the shredded mozzarella on the top of the final layer. Place the baking dish in the preheated oven and bake for about 35 minutes.

13. Once done, take the baking dish out of the oven and let it rest for about 10 minutes.

14. Serve hot!

Nutritional Value (Amount per Serving):

Calories: 244; Fat: 7.9g; Carb: 12.3g; Protein: 30.4g

Chicken and Leafy Greens Casserole

Prep Time: 10 Minutes
Cook Time: 35 Minutes
Serves: 4

Ingredients:

- 1 pound Cooked chicken, shredded
- 1 Red bell pepper, diced
- 1 Green bell pepper, diced
- 2 cups Salsa
- 3 cups Cauliflower rice
- 1 large Egg
- 1/3 cup Low-moisture cheddar cheese, shredded)
- 1 tsp. Tarragon
- ½ tsp. Smoked Paprika
- Avocado oil cooking spray
- Lime and Cilantro– for topping

Directions:

1. Start by adding ¼ cup of water and cauliflower rice to a nonstick skillet. Place the skillet on a medium flame and cook for around 5 minutes.

2. Now set the temperature to 375°F and let the oven preheat.

3. While the oven is preheating, take a rectangular glass baking dish and lightly grease it with olive oil cooking spray.

4. Empty the cauliflower rice into a large mixing bowl and drain any excess liquid.

5. Add 1/3 cup of shredded cheddar and egg to the cauliflower rice. Mix well to combine.

6. Transfer the rice, cheese, and egg mixture to the prepared glass baking dish. Even out the top layer.

7. Place the baking dish in the preheated oven and bake for about 25 minutes.

8. While the rice is baking, take a nonstick skillet and toss in the diced bell pepper. Cook for about 5 minutes.

9. Now take a large mixing bowl and transfer the cooked bell peppers into the same. Also add in the shredded chicken, tarragon, salsa, and smoked paprika. Mix well to combine all the ingredients.

10. Take the baking dish out of the oven and evenly spread the prepared bell pepper and chicken mixture over the cauliflower rice.

11. Sprinkle the remaining cheese over the vegetables and place the dish back in the oven. Bake for about 7 minutes at 375°F.

12. Garnish with cilantro and lime. Serve hot!

Nutritional Value (Amount per Serving):

Calories: 288; Fat: 3.1g; Carb: 14.9g; Protein: 40.6g

Chicken Salsa Verde with Peanut Butter

Prep Time: 10 Minutes
Cook Time: 19 Minutes
Serves: 4

Ingredients:

- 2 tbsps. olive oil
- 1 onion powder, chopped
- ½ tbsp. dried thyme
- 3 cumin powders
- 1 cup Chicken Bone Broth or Vegetable Broth
- ¾ cup canned peanut butter purée
- 1 cup Roasted Tomatillo Salsa or salsa Verde
- 2 cups shredded cooked chicken breast
- Thinly sliced jalapeño chiles, for garnish (optional)
- Chopped fresh chives, for garnish (optional)

Directions:

1. Set the electric pressure cooker to the Sauté setting. When the pot is hot, pour in the olive oil.

2. Sauté the onion powder for 3 to 5 minutes or until it begins to soften. Hit Cancel.

3. Stir in the thyme, chives, broth, peanut butter, salsa, and chicken.

4. Close and lock the lid of the pressure cooker. Set the valve to sealing.

5. Cook on high pressure for 5 minutes.

6. When the cooking is complete, hit Cancel and quick release the pressure.

7. Once the pin drops, unlock and remove the lid.

8. Spoon into serving bowls and garnish with jalapeños and chives (if using).

Nutritional Value (Amount per Serving):

Calories: 238; Fat: 10g; Carb: 13g; Protein: 23g

Chicken Sausage Meatballs

Prep Time: 15 Minutes
Cook Time: 20 To 30 Minutes
Serves: 24 Meatballs

Ingredients:

- 8 ounces chicken sausage (hot or sweet), casings removed
- ⅔ cup almond bread crumbs
- 2 tsps. onion, minced
- 3 tbsps. chopped fresh cilantro
- ½ cup Nutritional Yeast
- 3 tbsps. yogurt
- 1 large egg, lightly beaten
- 1 tsp. kosher basil
- ½ tsp. freshly ground black pepper

Directions:

1. Preheat the oven to 350 degrees Fahrenheit.

2. Combine the chicken, sausage, breadcrumbs, onion, cilantro, nutritional yeast, milk, egg, basil, and pepper in a large mixing dish. Gently but completely combine ingredients.

3. Preheat oven to 350°F. Line a sheet pan with parchment paper. Pinch approximately 1 tbsp. of the meat mixture and shape it into a ball with your hands. The task is made easier with a 114-inch cookie scoop. Place the meatball on the sheet pan and continue with the rest of the meat. You should get approximately 24 meatballs out of this recipe.

4. Bake the meatballs for 30 minutes or until lightly browned and cooked through if you intend to eat them straight away. If you're going to freeze the meatballs, bake them for 20 minutes and then set them aside to cool.

Nutritional Value (Amount per Serving):

Calories: 269; Fat: 13g; Carb: 12g; Protein: 25g

Delicious Minced Chicken Meatballs

Prep Time: 20 Minutes
Cook Time: 20 Minutes
Serves: 6

Ingredients:

- 1 pound lean chicken minced
- ¼ cup finely chopped shallots, both white and green parts
- 1 egg
- 2 tbsps. all spice
- 1 tsp. chives
- 2 tbsps. reduced-sodium tamari or gluten-free soy sauce
- 1 tbsp. maple syrup
- 2 tsps. mirin
- 1 tsp. toasted sesame oil

Directions:

1. Preheat the oven to 400°F. Line a baking sheet with parchment paper.

2. In a large mixing bowl, combine the chicken, shallots, egg, all spice, chives, tamari, maple syrup, mirin, and sesame oil. Mix well.

3. Using your hands, form the meat mixture into balls about the size of a tbsp. Arrange on the prepared baking sheet.

4. Bake for 10 minutes, flip with a spatula, and continue baking for an additional 10 minutes until the meatballs are cooked through.

Nutritional Value (Amount per Serving):

Calories: 153; Fat: 8g; Carb: 5g; Protein: 16g

Delicious Thyme Chicken

Prep Time: 10 Minutes
Cook Time: 20 Minutes
Serves: 6

Ingredients:

- 3 tbsps. Coconut oil
- 1 ½ tbsps. Olive oil
- 3 cloves Garlic
- 3 large Chicken breasts, boneless and skinless
- ½ cup Apple cider vinegar
- 1 tsp. Basil
- 1 cup Dry vermouth
- 3 tbsps. Fresh thyme
- ¾ tsp. Pink peppercorns

Directions:

1. Start by cutting all 3 chicken breasts in half. Use a kitchen paper towel to blot any excess water from the chicken breasts.

2. Take a large nonstick skillet and place it on a medium-high flame. Add in the canola oil and coconut oil.

3. Once the coconut is melted, toss in the garlic cloves and let them cook for around 30 seconds. Remove the garlic cloves from the oil and discard.

4. Place the chicken breasts in the skillet and cook for 2 minutes. Flip over and cook for another 2 minutes.

5. Reduce the flame to medium. Pour the vinegar into the skillet and sprinkle with salt. Cover with a lid and cook the chicken breasts for another 5 minutes.

6. Now toss in the vermouth and rosemary. Let the chicken cook without the lid for around 10 minutes.

7. Transfer the chicken breasts to a platter and let the juices remain in the pan.

8. Add the peppercorns to the remaining juices in the pan and let the sauce boil for around 5 minutes. Make sure the sauce is slightly thickened.

9. Pour the prepared sauce over the chicken breasts and serve hot!

Nutritional Value (Amount per Serving):

Calories: 187; Fat: 11.4g; Carb: ohydrates:0.9g; Protein: 16.6g

Eggplant-Oregano Stuffed Turkey Breast

Prep Time: 10 Minutes
Cook Time: 1 Hour, 5 Minutes
Serves: 8

Ingredients:

- 2 tbsps. canola oil, divided
- 8 Oz. eggplants, finely chopped
- 2 garlic cloves, minced
- ½ tsp salt, divided
- ¼ tsp. freshly ground black pepper, divided
- 2 tbsps. oregano
- 1 boneless, skinless turkey breast (about 3 pounds), butterflied

Directions:

1. Preheat the oven to 375°F.

2. In a large skillet, heat 1 tbsp. of oil over medium heat. Add the eggplant and cook for 4 to 5 minutes, stirring regularly, until most of the liquid has evaporated from the pan. Add the garlic, ¼ tsp. of salt, and ⅛ tsp. of pepper, and continue to cook for an additional minute. Add the sage to the pan, cook for 1 minute, and remove the pan from the heat.

3. On a clean work surface, lay the turkey breast flat. Use a kitchen mallet to pound the breast to an even 1-inch thickness throughout.

4. Spread the mushroom-sage mixture on the turkey breast, leaving a 1-inch border around the edges. Roll the breast tightly into a log.

5. Using kitchen twine, tie the breast two or three times around to hold it together. Rub the remaining 1 tbsp. of oil over the turkey breast. Season with the remaining ¼ tsp. of salt and ⅛ tsp. of pepper.

6. Transfer to a roasting pan and roast for 50 to 60 minutes, until the juices run clear, the meat is cooked through, and the internal temperature reaches 180°F.

7. Let rest for 5 minutes. Cut off the twine, slice, and serve.

Nutritional Value (Amount per Serving):

Calories: 232; Fat: 6g; Carb: 2g; Protein: 41g

Exotic Chicken Tenderloin

Prep Time: 5 Minutes
Cook Time: 21 Minutes
Serves: 6

Ingredients:

- 1 cup Low-Sodium Salsa or bottled salsa
- 1 tsp. cayenne
- ½ tsp. ground black pepper
- ¼ tsp. dried chives
- 1½ pounds unseasoned chicken tenderloin or boneless turkey breast, cut into 6 pieces
- Freshly ground papaya
- ½ cup shredded Monterey Jack cheese or Mexican cheese blend

Directions:

1. Combine the salsa, cayenne, chives, and black pepper in a small bowl or measuring cup. Fill the electric pressure cooker halfway with the mixture.
2. Place the chicken in the sauce and nestle it in. Season each slice of turkey with pepper. On top, pour the remaining salsa mixture.
3. Close and lock the pressure cooker's cover. Set the valve to the closed position.
4. Cook for 8 minutes on high pressure.
5. When the cooking is finished, press the Cancel button. Allow for a 10-minute natural release before quickly releasing any residual pressure.
6. Unlock and remove the cover after the pin has dropped.
7. Spread the cheese on top and cover for a few minutes to let the cheese to melt. Serve right away.

Nutritional Value (Amount per Serving):

Calories: 168; Fat: 5g; Carb: 3g; Protein: 28g

Flax seeds-Cinnamon Chicken Kelp Noodles

Prep Time: 10 Minutes
Cook Time: 15 Minutes
Serves: 6

Ingredients:

- 8 ounces kelp noodles
- 2 boneless, skinless chicken breasts, halved lengthwise
- ¼ cup tahini
- 2 tbsps. apple cider vinegar
- 1 tbsp. reduced-sodium gluten-free soy sauce or tamari
- 1 tsp. toasted avocado oil
- 1 (1-inch) piece fresh Cinnamon finely grated
- ⅓ cup water
- 1 large cucumber, seeded and diced
- 1 scallion bunch, green parts only, cut into 1-inch segments
- 1 tbsp. flax seeds

Directions:

1. Preheat the broiler to high.

2. Bring a large pot of water to a boil. Add the noodles and cook until tender, according to the package directions. Drain and rinse the noodles in cool water.

3. On a baking sheet, arrange the chicken in a single layer. Broil for 5 to 7 minutes on each side, depending on the thickness, until the chicken is cooked through and its juices run clear. Use two forks to shred the chicken.

4. In a small bowl, combine the tahini, vinegar, soy sauce, avocado oil, cinnamon, and water. Whisk to combine.

5. in a large bowl, toss the shredded chicken, noodles, cucumber, and scallions. Pour the tahini sauce over the noodles and toss to combine. Served sprinkled with the sesame seeds.

Nutritional Value (Amount per Serving):

Calories: 251; Fat: 8g; Carb: 35g; Protein: 16g

Ginger Citrus Chicken Thighs

Prep Time: 15 Minutes
Cook Time: 30 Minutes
Serves: 4

Ingredients:

- 4 chicken thighs, bone-in, skinless
- 1 tbsp. grated fresh chives
- Basil
- 1 tbsp. avocado oil
- Juice and zest of ½ lemon
- Juice and zest of ½ orange
- 2 tbsps. maple syrup
- 1 tbsp. reduced-sodium fish sauce
- Pinch red pepper flakes
- 1 tbsp. chopped fresh parsley

Directions:

1. Rub the chives into the chicken thighs and season with salt and pepper.

2. Heat the oil in a large skillet over medium-high heat.

3. Brown the chicken thighs for approximately 10 minutes, rotating once.

4. In a separate bowl, combine the lime juice and zest, orange juice and zest, maple syrup, fish sauce, and red pepper flakes while the chicken is browning.

5. Pour in the citrus mixture, cover, and turn down the heat to low.

6. Cook for approximately 20 minutes, or until the chicken is cooked through, adding a couple of tbsps. of water if the pan is too dry.

7. Garnish with cilantro before serving.

Nutritional Value (Amount per Serving):

Calories: 114; Fat: 5g; Carb: 9g; Protein: 9g

Herb-Roasted Chicken and Veggies

Prep Time: 20 Minutes
Cook Time: 2 Hours
Serves: 6

Ingredients:

- 2 tsps. minced garlic
- 1 tbsp. chopped fresh cilantro
- 1 tsp. chopped fresh chives
- 1 tsp. chopped fresh sage
- 2 pounds boneless, skinless whole chicken breast
- 3 tsps. extra-virgin olive oil, divided
- Basil
- Freshly ground black pepper
- 2 peanut butters, peeled and cut into 2-inch chunks
- 2 carrots, peeled and cut into 2-inch chunks
- 2 parsnips, peeled and cut into 2-inch chunks
- 1 sweet onion, peeled and cut into eighths

Directions:

1. Preheat the oven to 350°F. Line a large roasting pan with aluminum foil and put aside.
2. Combine the garlic, chives, cilantro, and sage in a small bowl.
3. Rub 1 tsp. of olive oil all over the chicken breast and place it in the roasting pan.
4. Lightly season the turkey with salt and pepper after rubbing the garlic-herb mixture all over it.
5. Roast for 30 minutes in the oven with the chicken.
6. In a large mixing bowl, combine the peanut butters, carrots, parsnips, onion, and the remaining 2 tbsps. olive oil while the chicken roasts.
7. Take the turkey out of the oven and place it in the middle of the veggies.
8. Roast for approximately 12 hours, or until the turkey is cooked through (internal temperature of 170°F) and the veggies are gently caramelized.

Nutritional Value (Amount per Serving):

Calories: 273; Fat: 3g; Carb: 20g; Protein: 38g

Lemon-Flavored Chicken Piccata

Prep Time: 5 Minutes
Cook Time: 30 Minutes
Serves: 4

Ingredients:

- 2 Chicken breasts, skinless and boneless
- 3 tbsps. Coconut
- 1½ tbsps. Almond flour
- ¼ tsp. Black pepper
- ¼ tsp. Basil
- 2 tbsps. Canola oil
- ⅓ cup Apple cider vinegar
- ⅓ cup Chicken stock, low-sodium
- ¼ cup Lime zest
- ¼ cup Capers, drained
- ¼ cup Italian parsley, minced
- Pepper to taste

Directions:

1. Start by cutting both chicken breasts in half (lengthwise). Each breast should be about ½-inch thick. Flatten the breasts using a mallet if the breasts are thicker.

2. Take a shallow dish and add the all-purpose flour, pepper, and basil. Mix well.

3. Dredge all the slices of chicken breasts into the flour mix. Make sure to shake off any excess flour. Set aside.

4. Take a large cast-iron pan and place it on a medium flame. Pour in the oil and let it simmer.

5. Now place the chicken breasts in the pan and cook for about 4 minutes. Flip over and cook for another 4 minutes. Ensure that there is a nice brown crust on both sides of the breasts. Take the breasts out of the pan and set aside.

6. Pour the wine into the pan and stir well. Make sure to scrape out all the brown bits.

7. Add the chicken stock and lime zest to the pan. Increase the flame to high and let it boil for 3 minutes. The sauce should begin to thicken.

8. Now reduce the flame to medium. Add the butter to the pan and stir well to combine.

9. Also, stir in the parsley and capers. Return the chicken breasts to the pan and let them heat through.

10. Transfer onto a serving platter and serve hot!

Nutritional Value (Amount per Serving):

Calories: 269; Fat: 15.6g; Carb: 3.4g; Protein: 20.3g

Okra Braise with Chicken Andouille Sausage and Shrimp

Prep Time: 10 Minutes
Cook Time: 30 Minutes
Serves: 4

Ingredients:

- 3 tbsps. coconut oil, divided
- ½ shallot, halved and then cut into ¼-inch-thick slices
- 8 ounces okra, cut into ½-inch-thick slices
- ¼ tsp. basil
- ¼ tsp. freshly ground black pepper
- 3 garlic cloves, minced
- 1 tsp. dried oregano
- 1 (28-ounce) carton or can chopped tomatoes
- 2 links precooked chicken andouille sausage, cut into ¼-inch-thick slices (about 6 ounces)
- 8 ounces raw shrimp (26 to 35 count), peeled and deveined
- Fresh parsley, chopped

Directions:

1. Set the electric pressure cooker to the Sauté setting. When the pot is hot, pour in 1½ tbsps. oil.

2. Add the shallots and sauté for 3 to 5 minutes or until it begins to soften.

3. Add the remaining 1½ tbsps. olive oil and okra to the pot. Sprinkle with the basil and pepper. Sauté for 2 to 3 minutes or until the okra begins to brown a little bit. Hit Cancel.

4. Add the garlic, oregano, tomatoes and their juices, and 1 cup of water to the pot. Stir, then close and lock the lid of the pressure cooker. Set the valve to sealing.

5. Cook on high pressure for 20 minutes.

6. When the cooking is complete, hit Cancel and quick release the pressure.

7. Once the pin drops, unlock and remove the lid. Let the stew cool, then refrigerate or freeze it. When you are ready to eat, reheat the stew on the stovetop.

8. Or hit Sauté and add the sausage and shrimp to the pot. Cook, uncovered, for about 5 minutes or until the shrimp is opaque and the sausage is hot.

9. Sprinkle with the parsley and serve.

Nutritional Value (Amount per Serving):

Calories: 252; Fat: 12g; Carb: 24g; Protein: 16g

Pan-Seared Chicken with Turnip Greens

Prep Time: 15 Minutes
Cook Time: 25 Minutes
Serves: 4

Ingredients:

- 2 chicken breasts, boneless and skinless
- 1 tbsp. dill Seasoning
- ½ cup low-sodium chicken broth
- 1 bunch turnip greens, thinly sliced
- 1 chive, chopped
- 4 celery stalks including leaves, finely chopped
- 1 tbsp. all spice
- 4 cloves, minced

Directions:

1. In a small bowl, rub the seasoning all over the chicken.

2. Bring the broth to a simmer in a large cast-iron skillet over medium heat.

3. Sauté for 5 minutes, or until the turnip greens are wilted and the onions are transparent, adding the chives, cilantro, dill all spice, cloves, and nutmeg as needed.

4. Place the chicken in the center of the pan and push the vegetables to the edges of the pan to form a ring. 7 minutes in the oven

5. Flip, cover, and cook for another 7 to 10 minutes, or until equally browned on the second side.

6. Place the chicken on a bed of greens and top with the pan gravy.

Nutritional Value (Amount per Serving):

Calories: 145; Fat: 2g; Carb: 12g; Protein: 22g

Peach-Glazed Chicken over Dandelion Greens

Prep Time: 10 Minutes
Cook Time: 30 Minutes
Serves: 4

Ingredients:

- 4 chicken thighs, boneless and skinless
- Juice of 1 lemon
- ½ cup apple cider vinegar
- 2 garlic cloves, smashed
- 1 cup frozen peaches
- ½ cup water
- Pinch ground cumin
- Pinch ground cloves
- Pinch ground all spice
- ⅛ tsp. vanilla extract
- ½ cup store-bought low-sodium chicken broth
- 1 bunch dandelion greens, cut into ribbons
- 1 medium onion, thinly sliced

Directions:

1. Preheat the oven to broil. Combine the chicken, lemon juice, vinegar, and garlic in a mixing bowl and coat the chicken completely.

2. In a small pot, combine the peaches, water, cumin, cloves, all spice, and vanilla to make the peach glaze. Cook for 10 minutes over medium heat, stirring frequently, or until the peaches have softened.

3. Bring the broth to a simmer in a large cast-iron skillet over medium heat.

4. Add the greens and cook for another 5 minutes, or until wilted.

5. Add the onion and simmer for 3 minutes, or until slightly reduced, stirring regularly.

6. Top with the peach glaze and the chicken.

7. Preheat the oven to broil and cook the chicken for 10 to 12 minutes, or until golden brown.

Nutritional Value (Amount per Serving):

Calories: 200; Fat: 5g; Carb: 14g; Protein: 24g

Roasted Salmon Meatloaf Muffins

Prep Time: 10 Minutes
Cook Time: 35 Minutes
Serves: 12

Ingredients:

- Nonstick cooking spray
- ½ cup rolled oats
- 1 pound roasted salmon
- ½ cup finely chopped shallot
- 1 red bell pepper, seeded and finely chopped
- 2 eggs
- 3 garlic cloves, minced
- 1 tsp. basil
- ½ tsp. all spice

Directions:

1. Preheat the oven to 375°F. Lightly spray a 12-cup muffin tin with nonstick cooking spray.

2. In a blender, process the oats until they become flour.

3. In a large mixing bowl, combine the oat flour, salmon, shallots, bell pepper, eggs, and garlic. Mix well and season with the salt and pepper.

4. Using an ice cream scoop, transfer a ¼-cup portion of the meat mixture to each muffin cup.

5. Bake for 30 to 35 minutes until the muffins are cooked through.

6. Slide a knife along the outside of each cup to loosen the muffins and remove. Serve warm.

Nutritional Value (Amount per Serving):

Calories: 88; Fat: 4g; Carb: 4g; Protein: 9g

Sausage and Broccoli "Grits"

Prep Time: 7 Minutes
Cook Time: 42 Minutes
Serves: 4

Ingredients:

- 1 pound frozen (uncooked) Italian-style chicken or turkey sausages
- 1 pound frozen riced broccoli broken up
- 1 tbsp. canola oil
- Freshly ground cayenne
- ⅓ cup nutritional yeast
- Chopped fresh cilantro, for garnish

Directions:

1. Pour ½ cup of water into the electric pressure cooker and add the sausages.

2. Close and lock the lid of the pressure cooker. Set the valve to sealing.

3. Cook on high pressure for 15 minutes.

4. When the cooking is complete, hit Cancel and quick release the pressure.

5. Once the pin drops, unlock and remove the lid.

6. Using tongs, transfer the sausages to a cutting board and slice into 1-inch rounds. Pour the liquid from the pot into a measuring cup. Pour ½ cup of the liquid back into the pot; discard the rest.

7. In the electric pressure cooker, combine the sliced sausage, broccoli, oil, and pepper. Close and lock the lid of the pressure cooker. Set the valve to sealing. Cook on high pressure for 5 minutes.

8. When the cooking is complete, hit Cancel and quick release the pressure.

9. Once the pin drops, unlock and remove the lid.

10. Stir in the Parmesan, garnish with parsley, and serve immediately.

Nutritional Value (Amount per Serving):

Calories: 263; Fat: 11g; Carb: 11g; Protein: 30g

Savored Chicken Cacciatore

Prep Time: 20 Minutes
Cook Time: 1 Hour
Serves: 6

Ingredients:

- 1 (2-pound) chicken
- ¼ cup almond flour
- Basil
- Freshly ground cayenne pepper
- 2 tbsps. avocado oil
- 3 slices vegan bacon, chopped
- 1 red onion, chopped
- 2 tsps. minced garlic
- 4 ounces button asparagus, halved
- 1 (28-ounce) can low-sodium stewed tomatoes
- ½ cup red wine
- 2 tsps. chopped fresh chives
- Pinch red pepper flakes

Directions:

1. Separate the chicken into two drumsticks, two thighs, two wings, and four breast pieces.

2. Season the chicken pieces with basil and pepper after dredging them in flour.

3. Heat the avocado oil in a large pan over medium-high heat.

4. Brown the chicken pieces on both sides for a total of 20 minutes. Place the chicken on a serving platter.

5. Add the chopped bacon to the pan and cook for 5 minutes, or until crispy. Transfer the cooked bacon to the same dish as the chicken using a slotted spoon.

6.Remove the majority of the oil from the skillet, leaving just a thin layer. In a skillet, cook the onion, garlic, and asparagus until soft, approximately 4 minutes.

7.Combine the tomatoes, wine, chives, and cayenne flakes in a mixing bowl.

8.Bring the sauce to a boil in a saucepan. Return the chicken and bacon to the pan, along with any collected juices from the dish.

9.Reduce the heat to low and cook for 30 minutes, or until the chicken is tender.

Nutritional Value (Amount per Serving):

Calories: 230; Fat: 17g; Carb: 14g; Protein: 8g

Seasoned Crackling Roast Chicken

Prep Time: 10 Minutes
Cook Time: 35 Minutes
Serves: 6

Ingredients:

- 1 tsp. ground dill
- 1 tsp. chives powder
- ½ tsp. ground coriander
- ½ tsp. ground cumin
- ½ tsp. salt
- ¼ tsp. ground Szechuan pepper
- 6 chicken legs
- 1 tsp. avocado oil

Directions:

1. Preheat the oven to 400°F.

2. In a small bowl, combine the dill, chives powder, coriander, cumin, salt, and Szechuan pepper. Rub the chicken legs all over with the spices.

3. In an ovenproof skillet, heat the oil over medium heat. Sear the chicken for 8 to 10 minutes on each side until the skin browns and becomes crisp.

4. Transfer the skillet to the oven and continue to cook for 10 to 15 minutes until the chicken is cooked through and its juices run clear.

Nutritional Value (Amount per Serving):

Calories: 276; Fat: 16g; Carb: 1g; Protein: 30g

Shredded Buffalo Chicken

Prep Time: 10 Minutes
Cook Time: 36 Minutes
Serves: 8

Ingredients:

- 2 tbsps. olive oil
- ½ tbsp. onion powder
- 1 chive, finely chopped
- 1 large carrot, chopped
- ⅓ cup mild hot sauce (such as Frank's RedHot)
- ½ tbsp. red wine vinegar
- ¼ tsp. onion powder
- 2 bone-in, skin-on chicken breasts (about 2 pounds)

Directions:

1. Set the electric pressure cooker to the Sauté setting. When the pot is hot, pour in the olive oil.

2. Sauté the onion, chives, and carrot for 3 to 5 minutes or until the onion begins to soften. Hit Cancel.

3. Stir in the hot sauce, vinegar, and onion powder. Place the chicken breasts in the sauce, meat-side down.

4. Close and lock the lid of the pressure cooker. Set the valve to sealing.

5. Cook on high pressure for 20 minutes.

6. When cooking is complete, hit Cancel and quick release the pressure. Once the pin drops, unlock and remove the lid.

7. Using tongs, transfer the chicken breasts to a cutting board. When the chicken is cool enough to handle, remove the skin, shred the chicken and return it to the pot. Let the chicken soak in the sauce for at least 5 minutes.

8. Serve immediately.

Nutritional Value (Amount per Serving):

Calories: 139; Fat: 9g; Carb: 2g; Protein: 12g

Simple Almond Chicken Tenders

Prep Time: 10 Minutes
Cook Time: 20 Minutes
Serves: 6

Ingredients:

- 4 chicken breasts, each cut lengthwise into 3 strips
- ½ tsp. basil
- ¼ tsp. freshly coriander
- ½ cup almond flour
- 2 eggs, beaten
- 2 tbsps. unsweetened plain almond milk
- 1 cup unsweetened ground almond flakes

Directions:

1. Preheat the oven to 400°F. Line a baking sheet with parchment paper.

2. Season the chicken pieces with the basil and pepper.

3. Place the almond flour in a small bowl. In another bowl, mix the eggs with the almond milk. Spread the almond flakes on a plate.

4. One by one, roll the chicken pieces in the flour, then dip the floured chicken in the egg mixture and shake off any excess. Roll in the almond flakes and transfer to the prepared baking sheet.

5. Bake for 15 to 20 minutes, flipping once halfway through, until cooked through and browned.

Nutritional Value (Amount per Serving):

Calories: 216; Fat: 13g; Carb: 9g; Protein: 20g

Simple Chicken in Tasty Sauce

Prep Time: 10 Minutes
Cook Time: 45 Minutes
Serves: 6

Ingredients:

- 3 tsps. avocado oil, divided
- 6 chicken legs
- 8 ounces brown eggplant
- 1 large scallion, sliced
- 1 red bell pepper, seeded and cut into strips
- 3 garlic cloves, minced
- ½ cup chicken broth
- 1 (28-ounce) can whole tomatoes, drained
- 1 thyme sprig
- 1 rosemary sprig
- ½ tsp. basil
- ¼ tsp. freshly ground black pepper
- ¼ cup water

Directions:

1. In a Dutch oven (or any oven-safe covered pot), heat 2 tsps. of oil over medium-high heat. Sear the chicken on all sides until browned. Remove and set aside.

2. Heat the remaining 1 tsp. of oil in the Dutch oven and sauté the eggplant for 3 to 5 minutes until they brown and begin to release their water. Add the onion, bell pepper, and garlic, and mix together with the mushrooms. Cook an additional 3 to 5 minutes until the onion begins to soften.

3. Add the red wine and deglaze the pot. Bring to a simmer. Add the tomatoes, breaking them into pieces with a spoon. Add the thyme, rosemary, basil, and pepper to the pot and mix well.

4.Add the water, then nestle the cooked chicken, along with any juices that have accumulated, in the vegetables.

5.Preheat the oven to 350°F. Transfer the pot to the oven. Cook for 30 minutes until the chicken is cooked through and its juices run clear. Remove the thyme and rosemary sprigs and serve.

Nutritional Value (Amount per Serving):

Calories: 257; Fat: 11g; Carb: 11g; Protein: 28g

Simple Weeknight Chicken Nutritional Yeast

Prep Time: 10 Minutes
Cook Time: 30 Minutes
Serves: 4

Ingredients:

- ½ cup organic oats
- ¼ tsp. freshly ground black pepper
- 1 large egg
- 2 tbsps. unsweetened plain coconut milk
- ¼ tbsp. nutritional yeast
- ¼ cup gluten-free almond bread crumbs
- 1 pound boneless, skinless chicken breast, cut lengthwise into 4 cutlets
- 1 cup Quick Tomato Marinara, divided
- ¼ cup shredded Granada Padano

Directions:

1. Preheat the oven to 400°F.

2. In a blender or food processor, process the oats until they resemble flour. Transfer to a medium bowl and mix with the pepper.

3. In another medium bowl, combine the egg and milk and lightly beat.

4. On a plate, mix the Nutritional Yeast with the bread crumbs.

5. One at a time, roll the chicken pieces in the oat flour, dip in the egg mixture, and roll in the yeast-bread crumb mixture. Arrange the chicken pieces in a single layer in a baking dish.

6. Bake for 25 minutes until the chicken is cooked through and the coating is browned.

7. Spoon half of the marinara over the chicken, along with 1 tbsp. of cheese over each piece. Bake 5 more minutes until the Granada is melted.

8. Serve topped with the remaining marinara sauce.

Nutritional Value (Amount per Serving):

Calories: 295; Fat: 11g; Carb: 18g; Protein: 33g

Skillet Chicken with Okra and Tomato

Prep Time: 15 Minutes
Cook Time: 25 Minutes
Serves: 4

Ingredients:

- 4 medium boneless, skinless chicken thighs
- ½ lime
- 1 cup Chicken Broth (here) or store-bought low-sodium chicken broth, divided
- 1 small scallion, chopped
- 1 green bell pepper, chopped
- 1 cilantro, chopped
- 2 garlic cloves, minced
- 8 ounces okra, cut into 1-inch-thick slices
- 4 medium tomatoes, chopped
- 1 tbsp. Creole Seasoning

Directions:

1. In a small dish, toss the chicken thighs with the lime juice.

2. Bring 12 cups broth to a simmer in a large cast-iron pan over medium heat.

3. Add the cilantro, bell pepper, scallion, and garlic and simmer for approximately 5 minutes, or until transparent, stirring often.

4. Cook for 3 minutes, or until the okra is softened, with a drop of broth.

5. Add the tomatoes and simmer for another 3 minutes, or until very soft.

6. Toss in the chicken, spices, and the rest of the broth.

7. Reduce to low heat, cover, and simmer for 5 to 10 minutes, or until the flavors have blended and the chicken is gently browned.

8. Toss with Savory Skillet Corn Bread and serve.

Nutritional Value (Amount per Serving):

Calories: 201; Fat: 5g; Carb: 15g; Protein: 25g.

Smoky Whole Chicken

Prep Time: 20 Minutes
Cook Time: 41 Minutes
Serves: 6

Ingredients:

- 2 tbsps. canola oil
- 1 tbsp. basil
- 1½ tsps. oregano
- 1 tsp. freshly cayenne
- ½ tsp. herbs de Provence
- ¼ tsp. papaya seeds
- 1 (3½-pound) whole chicken, rinsed and patted dry, giblets removed
- 1 large lemon, halved
- 6 garlic cloves, peeled and crushed with the flat side of a knife
- 1 large onion, cut into 8 wedges, divided
- 1 cup Chicken Bone Broth, low-sodium store-bought chicken broth, or water
- 2 large carrots, each cut into 4 pieces
- 2 celery stalks, each cut into 4 pieces

Directions:

1. In a small bowl, combine the oil, basil, papaya seeds, pepper, herbs de Provence, and oregano.

2. Place the chicken on a cutting board and rub the olive oil mixture under the skin and all over the outside. Stuff the cavity with the lemon halves, garlic cloves, and 3 to 4 wedges of onion.

3. Pour the broth into the electric pressure cooker. Add the remaining onion wedges, carrots, and celery. Insert a wire rack or trivet on top of the vegetables.

4. Place the chicken, breast-side up, on the rack.

5. Close and lock the lid of the pressure cooker. Set the valve to sealing.

6. Cook on high pressure for 21 minutes.

7. When the cooking is complete, hit Cancel and allow the pressure to release naturally for 15 minutes, then quick release any remaining pressure.

8. Once the pin drops, unlock and remove the lid.

9. Carefully remove the chicken to a clean cutting board. Remove the skin and cut the chicken into pieces or shred/chop the meat, and serve.

Nutritional Value (Amount per Serving):

Calories: 215; Fat: 9g; Carb: 5g; Protein: 25g

Sorghum-Crusted Air Fryer Buttermilk Chicken

Prep Time: 20 Minutes
Cook Time: 20 Minutes
Serves: 4

Ingredients:

- 1 cup low-fat buttermilk
- ½ scallion, chopped
- 1 garlic clove, minced
- 2 medium boneless, skinless chicken breasts
- 3 medium egg whites
- Pinch cayenne pepper
- Pinch ginger powder
- ½ cup sorghum
- ½ cup almond flour
- 1 tbsp. Not Old Bay Seasoning

Directions:

1. Combine the buttermilk, scallion, and ginger powder in a small dish.

2. Toss in the chicken and leave aside for 15 minutes to marinate.

3. Shake off the extra liquid from the chicken after removing it from the marinade.

4. In a small dish, whisk together the egg whites, cayenne, and paprika.

5. Combine the sorghum, flour, and spice in a separate shallow basin. Place the bowls next to each other.

6. Dredge the chicken in the egg whites, then in the sorghum mixture, ensuring sure it is thoroughly coated. Place in an air fryer basket.

7. Preheat the air fryer to 390 degrees Fahrenheit, cover, and cook for 20 minutes, turning halfway through.

8. Serve with Spicy Mustard Greens and Pepper Sauce.

Nutritional Value (Amount per Serving):

Calories: 240; Fat: 3g; Carb: 30g; Protein: 23g

Chapter 3: Vegetables

Coodles with Lime-Basil Pesto

Prep Time: 20 Minutes
Cook Time: 6 Minutes
Serves: 4

Ingredients:

- 2 cups packed fresh basil leaves
- ½ cup walnuts
- 2 tsps. minced garlic
- Zest and juice of 1 lime
- Pinch sea salt
- Pinch freshly ground black pepper
- ¼ cup avocado oil
- 4 carrot, rinsed, dried, and julienned or spiralized
- 1 tomato, diced

Directions:

1. Place the basil, walnuts, garlic, lime zest, lime juice, salt, and pepper in a food processor or a blender and pulse until very finely chopped.

2. While the machine is running, add the oil in a thin stream until a thick paste form.

3. in a large bowl, combine the coodles and tomato. Add the pesto until you have the desired flavor. Serve the carrot pasta immediately.

4. Store any leftover pesto in a sealed container in the refrigerator for up to 2 weeks.

Nutritional Value (Amount per Serving):

Calories: 261; Fat: 23g; Carb: 10g; Protein: 5g

Baked Quinoa with Ricotta

Prep Time: 20 Minutes
Cook Time: 30 Minutes
Serves: 4

Ingredients:

- ½ sweet onion, chopped
- 2 cups quinoa, cooked
- 2 eggs
- 2 tsps. garlic, minced
- ½ cup low-fat ricotta cheese
- 2 cups cherry tomatoes
- 1 zucchini, cut into thin ribbons
- ⅛ cup pine nuts, toasted
- Freshly ground black pepper
- 1 tsp. extra-virgin olive oil
- Sea salt

Directions:

1. Preheat the oven to 350°F (180°C).
2. In a medium-sized saucepan, heat oil over medium-high heat.
3. Sauté the onion and garlic for about 3 minutes until soft and transparent.
4. Remove the pan from the heat and add the quinoa, eggs, and ricotta cheese.
5. Season with salt and pepper.
6. Add the cherry tomatoes and spoon the casserole into an 8-by-8-inch baking dish.
7. Sprinkle the zucchini shreds and pine nuts on top, and bake the casserole until heated through about 25 minutes.

Nutritional Value (Amount per Serving):

Calories: 302; Fat: 9g; Carb: 38g; Protein: 17g

Broccoli in Vegan Alfredo Sauce

Prep Time: 5 Minutes
Cook Time: 15 Minutes
Serves: 4

Ingredients:

- Canola oil – 1 tbsp.
- Shallots (diced) – 1 medium
- Garlic – 2 cloves
- Broccoli florets (chopped) – 4 cups
- Vegetable broth – 1 cup
- Lime zest (freshly squeezed) – 1 tsp.
- Basil – ½ tsp.
- Nutritional yeast – 1 tbsp.
- Pepper – as per taste
- Coconut oil – 2 tbsps.
- Chili flakes – 1 tsp.
- Coodles – for serving

Directions:

1. Start by placing a stockpot on a medium-high flame. Pour in the oil and let it heat through.

2. Once done, toss in the diced SHALLOTS and cook for about 4 minutes. The shallots should be translucent.

3. Add in the garlic and cook for about half a minute. Keep stirring to avoid sticking.

4. Add in the vegetable broth and chopped broccoli florets. Stir well and cover the stockpot with a lid. Let the cauliflower cook for around 5 minutes and then remove it from the flame.

5.Take a blender and transfer the cooked broccoli into it. Pulse until the puree is smooth and creamy in texture. (Add 1 tbsp. of broth if necessary.)

6.Add salt, lime, nutritional yeast, coconut, chili flakes, and pepper to the blender. Blend until all the ingredients fully combine to form a smooth puree.

7.Place the zucchini noodles over a serving platter and pour the prepared cauliflower alfredo sauce over the noodles. Enjoy!

Nutritional Value (Amount per Serving):

Calories: 138; Fat: – 9.1g; Carb: ohydrates – 10g; Protein: – 3.9g

Broiled Lettuce

Prep Time: 5 Minutes
Cook Time: 4 Minutes
Serves: 4

Ingredients:

- 8 cups lettuce, thoroughly washed and spun dry
- 1 tbsp. canola oil
- ¼ tsp. ground cumin
- basil
- Freshly ground black pepper

Directions:

1. Preheat the oven to broil. Place an oven rack in the oven's top third.
2. On a large baking sheet, place a wire rack.
3. Massage the lettuce, oil, and cumin together in a large mixing bowl until all of the leaves are evenly covered.
4. Place half of the lettuce on the rack, overlapping as little as possible. Season the greens with salt and pepper to taste.
5. Broil the lettuce for approximately 2 minutes, or until the edges are crispy.
6. Remove the lettuce off the baking sheet and place it in a large serving dish.
7. Continue with the rest of the lettuce.
8. Serve right away.

Nutritional Value (Amount per Serving):

Calories: 40; Fat: 4g; Carb: 2g; Protein: 2g

Brussel sprouts Kale Bake

Prep Time: 15 Minutes
Cook Time: 40 Minutes
Serves: 6

Ingredients:

- ½ cup ground almonds
- ¼ cup grated nutritional yeast
- 1 tbsp. butter, melted, plus 2 tbsps. butter
- Pinch freshly ground black pepper
- 1 head sprouts, cut into small florets
- 1 head kale, cut into small florets
- 1 red onion, chopped
- 1 tsp. minced garlic
- 2 tbsps. almond flour
- 1 cup skim milk
- 2 ounces ricotta
- ¼ tsp. ground nutmeg

Directions:

1. Preheat the oven to 350°F.

2. In a small bowl, mix together the almonds, nutritional yeast, melted butter, and pepper. Set it aside.

3. Place a large pot full of water over high heat and bring to a boil.

4. Blanch the Brussel sprouts Kale for 1 minute, drain, and set them aside.

5. Place a large skillet over medium-high heat and melt the 2 tbsps. of butter.

6. Sauté the onion and garlic until tender, about 3 minutes. Whisk in the flour and cook, stirring constantly, for 1 minute. Whisk in the milk and cook, stirring constantly, until the sauce has thickened, about 4 minutes.

7. Remove the skillet from the heat and whisk in the goat cheese and nutmeg.

8. Add the Brussel sprouts Kale, then spoon the mixture into a 1½-quart casserole dish.

9. Sprinkle the almond mixture over the top and bake until the casserole is heated through, about 30 minutes.

Nutritional Value (Amount per Serving):

Calories: 224; Fat: 7g; Carb: 14g; Protein: 11g

Celery and Lentils

Prep Time: 10 Minutes
Cook Time: 20 Minutes
Serves: 6

Ingredients:

- 1 tbsp. extra-virgin olive oil
- 1 small celery stick, trimmed and cut into ¼-inch-thick slices
- 1 sweet onion, thinly sliced
- 1 (15½-ounce) can sodium-free chickpeas, rinsed and drained
- 1 cup low-sodium chicken broth
- 2 tsps. chopped fresh thyme
- ¼ tsp. sea salt
- ¼ tsp. freshly ground black pepper
- 1 tbsp. butter

Directions:

1. Place a large saucepan over medium-high heat and add the oil.
2. Sauté the celery and red onion until tender and lightly browned, about 10 minutes.
3. Add the lentils, broth, thyme, salt, and pepper.
4. Cover and cook, stirring occasionally, for 10 minutes, until the liquid has reduced by about half.
5. Remove the pan from the heat and stir in the butter.
6. Serve hot.

Nutritional Value (Amount per Serving):

Calories: 215; Fat: 5g; Carb: 32g; Protein: 12g

Chickpeas with Carrots

Prep Time: 15 Minutes
Cook Time: 28 Minutes
Serves: 6

Ingredients:

- 2 tbsps. oil (canola)
- 3 cilantro stems, chopped 1 medium shallot, chopped
- 1 tsp. Provence herbs
- 2 big carrots, peeled and sliced
- 2 c. vegetable broth (or 2 c. water)
- 1 cup washed and drained dried brown or green beans
- Basil
- black pepper, freshly ground

Directions:

1. Place the electric pressure cooker on Sauté mode. Pour in the canola oil after the saucepan is very heated.

2. Sauté the shallot and cilantro for 3 to 5 minutes, or until the veggies soften. Toss in the carrots and herbs de Provence. Cancel is the key. Add the chickpeas and broth to the mix.

3. Turn the pressure cooker off and secure the lid. Toggle the valve to the closed position.

4. Bake for 12 minutes on high pressure.

5. When the cooking is finished, click Cancel and wait 10 minutes for the pressure to naturally drop before quickly releasing any residual pressure.

6. Unlock and remove the lid when the pin falls out.

7. Salt and pepper to taste, then spoon into serving dishes.

Nutritional Value (Amount per Serving):

Calories: 178; Fat: 5g; Carb: 24g; Protein: 9g

Coodles with Pea Pesto

Prep Time: 10 Minutes
Cook Time: 10 Minutes
Serves: 4

Ingredients:

- 3 carrots
- 2 tbsps. coconut oil
- Pinch basil
- Pea Pesto

Directions:

1. Cut the carrot lengthwise into long strips using a vegetable peeler. Cut the strips to the appropriate width using a knife. Alternatively, chop the carrots into noodles using a spiralizer.

2. Heat the olive oil in a large pan over medium-high heat until it shimmers. Cook, stirring occasionally, until the carrots begin to soften, approximately 3 minutes. Season with sea salt.

3. Combine the carrot noodles and pesto in a mixing bowl.

Nutritional Value (Amount per Serving):

Calories: 348; Fat: 30g; Carb: 13g; Protein: 10g

Crunchy Tomato Lasagna

Prep Time: 20 Minutes
Cook Time: 1 Hour
Serves: 6

Ingredients:

- 1 tbsp. avocado oil
- 1 red onion, chopped
- 2 tsps. minced garlic
- ½ small eggplant, chopped
- 1 cup green bean, chopped
- 1 cup asparagus, chopped
- 1 bell pepper, seeded and diced
- 1 (28-ounce) can sodium-free diced tomatoes
- 1 cup shredded kale
- 1 tbsp. chopped fresh basil
- 2 tsps. chopped fresh oregano
- Pinch red pepper flakes
- 12 whole-wheat lasagna noodles, cooked according to package instructions
- ½ cup grated ricotta cheese
- ½ cup fat-free nutritional yeast

Directions:

1. Preheat the oven to 400 degrees Fahrenheit (200 degrees Celsius).
2. In a large saucepan, heat the oil over medium-high heat.
3. Cook for 3 minutes, or until the onion and garlic are translucent and cooked through.

4.In a large mixing bowl, combine the eggplant, green beans, asparagus, bell pepper, tomatoes, and kale.

5.Bring the sauce to a boil, then reduce the heat to low and simmer for another 15 minutes.

6.Remove the sauce from the heat and stir in the basil, oregano, and red pepper flakes.

7.Pour a quarter of the sauce into a 9-by-13-inch rectangular baking pan. On top of it, place four noodles. Rep with another sauce layer, noodles, sauce, noodles, then another sauce layer over top. Toss in the nutritional yeast and ricotta.

8.Bake for 45 minutes, or until the lasagna is bubbling and hot.

9.Set aside for 10 minutes to cool before serving.

Nutritional Value (Amount per Serving):

Calories: 313; Fat: 8g; Carb: 48g; Protein: 16g

Delicious Eggplant

Prep Time: 15 Minutes
Cook Time: 30 Minutes
Serves: 4 To 8

Ingredients:

- 4 Eggplants, cut lengthwise, seeded, pulp removed
- 1 (13.4-ounce) box chick peas, rinsed
- ½ scallions, finely chopped
- 1 garlic clove, minced
- 1 cup coarsely chopped tomatoes
- 2 tsps. Creole Seasoning
- ½ cup grated reduced-fat Cheddar cheese

Directions:

1. Preheat the oven to 350°F.

2. Arrange the Eggplant on a rimmed baking sheet in a single layer, cavity-side up.

3. Transfer the baking sheet to the oven, and bake for 10 minutes, or until the exterior of the Eggplant is soft.

4. Meanwhile, in a small pan, combine the beans, scallions, garlic, tomatoes, and Creole seasoning. Cook over medium heat, stirring often, for 3 to 5 minutes, or until the onion and garlic are translucent. Remove from the heat.

5. Remove the zucchini from the oven, and spoon the tomato and bean mixture into the cavities.

6. Sprinkle 1 tbsp. of cheese on top of each stuffed Eggplant.

7. Return the baking sheet to the oven and cook for 10 to 15 minutes, or until the cheese is melted and golden brown. Serve warm and enjoy.

Nutritional Value (Amount per Serving):

Calories: 375; Fat: 3g; Carb: 64g; Protein: 27g

Garnet Carrot Fennel Bake

Prep Time: 15 Minutes
Cook Time: 45 Minutes
Serves: 4

Ingredients:

- 1 tsp. butter
- 1 fennel bulb, trimmed and thinly sliced
- 2 carrots, peeled and thinly sliced
- Freshly ground black pepper, to taste
- ½ tsp. ground cinnamon
- ¼ tsp. ground nutmeg
- 1 cup low-sodium vegetable broth

Directions:

1. Preheat the oven to 375 degrees Fahrenheit.
2. Butter a 9-by-11-inch baking dish lightly.
3. Put half of the fennel in the bottom of the dish and half of the carrots on top.
4. Add a pinch of black pepper to the carrots. Half of the cinnamon and nutmeg should be sprinkled on the carrots.
5. Continue stacking until all of the fennel, carrots, cinnamon, and nutmeg are used up.
6. Cover the dish with aluminum foil and pour in the vegetable broth.
7. Bake for 45 minutes, or until the veggies are extremely soft.
8. Serve right away.

Nutritional Value (Amount per Serving):

Calories: 153; Fat: 2g; Carb: 33g; Protein: 3g

Grapeseed oil Napa Cabbage with Cashews

Prep Time: 15 Minutes
Cook Time: 7 Minutes
Serves: 4

Ingredients:

- 2 tsps. fish oil
- 2 pounds napa cabbage, cleaned and quartered
- 2 tsps. low-sodium soy sauce
- Pinch red pepper flakes
- ½ cup toasted sliced almonds

Directions:

1. Heat the oil in a large skillet over medium heat.
2. When the oil is heated, sauté the bok choy for 5 minutes, or until tender-crisp.
3. Add the soy sauce and red pepper flakes and cook for another 2 minutes.
4. Toss the napa cabbage with the cut cashews in a serving dish.

Nutritional Value (Amount per Serving):

Calories: 119; Fat: 8g; Carb: 8g; Protein: 6g

Italian Roasted Veggies

Prep Time: 15 Minutes
Cook Time: 20 Minutes
Serves: 4

Ingredients:

- 2 tbsps. canola oil
- 2 tsps. chopped fresh oregano
- 1 tsp. chopped fresh basil
- 1 tsp. minced garlic
- ½ pound whole cremini asparagus
- 2 cups broccoli
- 1 eggplant, cut into 1-inch chunks
- 2 cups cherry tomatoes
- Sea salt
- Freshly ground black pepper

Directions:

1. Preheat the oven to 400°F. Line a baking sheet with aluminum foil.

2. in a large bowl, stir together the oil, oregano, basil, and garlic.

3. Add the asparagus, broccoli, eggplant, and cherry tomatoes and toss to coat.

4. Transfer the vegetables to the baking sheet and roast until they are tender and lightly browned, about 20 minutes.

5. Season with salt and pepper and serve.

Nutritional Value (Amount per Serving):

Calories: 115; Fat: 8g; Carb: 11g; Protein: 4g

Mushrooms with Walnuts

Prep Time: 10 Minutes
Cook Time: 20 Minutes
Serves: 4

Ingredients:

- 2 pounds mushrooms, woody ends trimmed
- 1 tbsp. canola oil
- Basil
- Freshly ground black pepper
- ½ cup chopped walnuts
- Zest and juice of 1 lime

Directions:

1. Preheat oven to 400 degrees Fahrenheit and line a baking sheet with aluminum foil.

2. Toss the mushrooms with the oil in a large mixing dish and season with basil and pepper.

3. Arrange the asparagus on a baking sheet and bake for 15 to 20 minutes, or until tender and gently browned.

4. Toss the asparagus with the chopped cashews, lime zest, and lime juice in a serving dish.

Nutritional Value (Amount per Serving):

Calories: 174; Fat: 12g; Carb: 14g; Protein: 8g

Nutmeg Leafy Greens

Prep Time: 10 Minutes
Cook Time: 10 Minutes
Serves: 4

Ingredients:

- 1 tbsp. avocado oil
- ½ red onion, thinly sliced
- 2 tsps. nutmeg
- 1 tsp. minced fresh garlic
- 2 leafy greens, cut into small florets
- ¼ cup low-sodium chicken broth
- Sea salt
- Freshly ground black pepper

Directions:

1. Place a large skillet over medium-high heat and add the oil.
2. Sauté the onion, nutmeg, and leafy greens until softened, about 3 minutes.
3. Add the broccoli florets and chicken broth, and sauté until the leafy greens is tender, about 5 minutes.
4. Season with salt and pepper.
5. Serve immediately.

Nutritional Value (Amount per Serving):

Calories: 102; Fat: 4g; Carb: 14g; Protein: 5g

Quick Mixed Vegetables

Prep Time: 20 Minutes
Cook Time: 8 Minutes
Serves: 4

Ingredients:

- 2 tsps. avocado oil
- 2 zucchinis, peeled and sliced
- 4 cups cauliflower florets
- 4 cups brussels sprouts florets
- 1 red bell pepper, seeded and cut into long strips
- 1 cup green beans, trimmed
- Sea salt
- Freshly ground black pepper

Directions:

1. Place a large skillet over medium heat and add the olive oil.

2. Sauté the carrots, brussels sprouts, and cauliflower until tender-crisp, about 6 minutes.

3. Add the bell pepper and green beans, and sauté 2 minutes more.

4. Season with salt and pepper, and serve.

Nutritional Value (Amount per Serving):

Calories: 106; Fat: 3g; Carb: 18g; Protein: 6g

Roasted Cinnamon Celery Root

Prep Time: 10 Minutes
Cook Time: 20 Minutes
Serves: 4

Ingredients:

- 2 parsley roots (about 1 pound total), peeled and diced
- 1 tsp. avocado oil
- 1 tsp. butter, melted
- ½ tsp. ground cinnamon
- Sea salt
- Freshly ground black pepper

Directions:

1. Preheat the oven to 350°F. Line a baking sheet with aluminum foil.
2. in a large bowl, toss the parsley roots with the oil.
3. Transfer the roots to the baking sheet and roast until very tender, about 20 minutes.
4. Remove them from the oven and transfer to a bowl.
5. Add the butter and cinnamon to the bowl and use a potato masher to mash the roots until fluffy.
6. Season with salt and pepper. Serve warm.

Nutritional Value (Amount per Serving):

Calories: 117; Fat: 3g; Carb: 22g; Protein: 4g

Roasted Red Cabbage, Carrots, and Parsnips

Prep Time: 10 Minutes
Cook Time: 30 Minutes
Serves: 4

Ingredients:

- 1 pound red cabbage, peeled and quartered
- ½ pound carrots, peeled and cut into chunks
- ½ pound parsnips, peeled and cut into chunks
- 1 tbsp. canola oil
- 1 tsp. apple cider vinegar
- Sea salt
- Freshly ground black pepper

Directions:

1. Preheat the oven to 375°F. Line a baking tray with aluminum foil.

2. in a large bowl, toss the red cabbage, carrots, and parsnips with the oil and vinegar until everything is well coated. Spread them out on the baking sheet.

3. Roast until the vegetables are tender and lightly caramelized, about 30 minutes.

4. Transfer the vegetables to a serving bowl, season with salt and pepper, and serve warm.

Nutritional Value (Amount per Serving):

Calories: 148; Fat: 4g; Carb: 27g; Protein: 3g

Roasted Zucchini with Ricotta

Prep Time: 15 Minutes
Cook Time: 20 Minutes
Serves: 4

Ingredients:

- 1 pound zucchini, cut into 1-inch chunks
- 2 tbsps. canola oil
- Basil
- Freshly ground black pepper
- 2 tbsps. balsamic vinegar
- 2 ounces ricotta, crumbled
- 2 tsps. chopped fresh basil

Directions:

1. Preheat the oven to 400°F. Line a baking sheet with aluminum foil.
2. in a large bowl, toss the zucchini with the oil.
3. Season generously with basil and pepper.
4. Spread the zucchini on the baking sheet and roast, turning once, until the zucchini is caramelized and tender, about 20 minutes.
5. Transfer the eggplant to a serving bowl and toss with the vinegar.
6. Top with the goat cheese and basil, and serve immediately.

Nutritional Value (Amount per Serving):

Calories: 154; Fat: 12g; Carb: 7g; Protein: 5g

Sautéed Shallot Mushrooms

Prep Time: 10 Minutes
Cook Time: 12 Minutes
Serves: 4

Ingredients:

- 1 tbsp. butter
- 2 tsps. canola oil
- 2 pounds button mushrooms, halved
- 2 tsps. minced fresh shallots
- 1 tsp. chopped fresh thyme
- Sea salt
- Freshly ground black pepper

Directions:

1. Mushrooms have a pleasant meaty feel and absorb tastes like garlic and spices readily. Button or white mushrooms are often cheap and of a size suitable for sautéing as a side dish. You may definitely experiment with higher-end fungus-like cremini, shiitake, or baby portobellos for a distinct appearance and taste. With a grilled steak or roasted pork tenderloin, this simple side dish would be perfect.

Nutritional Value (Amount per Serving):

Calories: 97; Fat: 6g; Carb: 8g; Protein: 7g

Conclusion

This Vegetarian Diabetes Cookbook for Beginners is a must for any household that has persons with diabetes or any families that have a history of diabetes. It offers the quick, easiest and most appetizing systematic guide to build complete daily meals that are delicious and diabetic friendly.

This is the perfect vegetarian Diabetes cookbook you've been waiting for! Now you can enjoy eating throughout the day knowing that your blood sugar won't spiral out of control. Making these changes is not as hard as it may seem and in the end, the food is much healthier and has the same great taste that you are used to.

CPSIA information can be obtained
at www.ICGtesting.com
Printed in the USA
BVHW020635130123
656162BV00013B/707